LYNN BEDFORD HALL'S
NICE 'N EASY COOKBOOK

LYNN BEDFORD HALL'S
NICE 'N EASY
COOKBOOK

STRUIK

Struik Publishers (Pty) Ltd
(a member of The Struik Publishing Group (Pty) Ltd)
Cornelis Struik House
80 McKenzie Street
Cape Town
8001

Reg. No.: 54/00965/07

Copyright in text © Lynn Bedford Hall 1995
Copyright in photographs © Struik Publishers (Pty) Ltd 1995
Copyright in published edition © Struik Publishers (Pty) Ltd 1995

All rights reserved. No part of this publication may be reproduced, stored in a retrieval system, or transmitted, in any form or by any means, electronic, mechanical, photocopying, recording or otherwise, without the prior written permission of the copyright owners.

First published in 1995

Editor Sally Dicey
Cover designer Darren MacGurk
Designer Petal Palmer
Assistant Designer Lellyn Creamer
Photographer Anthony Johnson
Stylist Vo Pollard
Food preparation Annabel Ovenstone
Preparation of breads and biscuits Sylvia Grobbelaar
Preparation of cakes Cindy Dollery
Typesetting Struik DTP

Reproduction Hirt & Carter (Pty) Ltd, Cape Town
Printing and binding Kyodo Printing Co (Singapore) Pte Ltd

ISBN 1 86825 815 7

Author's acknowledgements

The credit for this book lies with a whole team of hardworking people, all deserving my thanks, but I have to be brief or you might give up reading this acknowledgement and miss the names I absolutely must highlight: editor, Sally Dicey; photographer, Anthony Johnson; cook and stylist, Vo Pollard. Sally has been the most patient, meticulous and considerate editor, checking the manuscript countless times, smoothing over hiccups, and fielding my relentless telephone calls cheerfully and expertly. Her dedication has been remarkable.

The photographs which leap from the pages are the result of the singular talents of Anthony and Vo. Their concept was brilliant: natural sunlight, beautiful pottery, leafy corners of Vo's Newlands garden - the results are simply an explosion of colour and exuberance. Their enthusiasm and energy never flagged, and their encouragement meant so much to me. Thank you sounds inadequate, for no author could wish for more:
this book is theirs as much as mine. My grateful thanks also to Petal Palmer, whose flair for design is apparent on every page, and then, of course, to publishing director and friend, Linda de Villiers. Without her the whole project might never have seen the light of day.

CONTENTS

Introduction 7

Starters 8

Soups 14

Fish and seafood 20

Meat 28

Poultry 34

Pasta 42

Vegetarian 48

Salads 54

Vegetables and grains 62

Desserts 66

Breads 78

Cakes 82

Sweet loaves 86

Biscuits 90

Index 95

MEASUREMENTS

Even though the weights of different kinds of flours differ slightly, I have, for the sake of convenience and because many cooks prefer using cups to scales, standardised 250 ml (1 cup) as equalling 120 g. The one exception is stoneground flour, which is much lighter than other wholewheat flours. Otherwise, the difference is not great enough to justify weighing out small quantities of grams.

What is important is to use a 250 ml cup and to weigh the ingredients once when starting to use this book, to make sure that you are using the correct metric cup, as they are NOT all the same size. You will find that the weights of most ingredients have been rounded off to the nearest convenient figure, to avoid the necessity of using a finely calibrated scale.

I have also standardised the weights of granulated, castor and golden brown sugar. Please note that soft brown and icing sugar are exceptions, both being lighter, cup for cup, than the others.

INTRODUCTION

Most of us who love to cook prefer to pitch our skills somewhere between the culinary extremes of frikkadels and Pâté de Foie Gras, and so I have written this book which, I think, carves a path down the middle. The recipes are neither too basic, nor too upmarket. They require no culinary embroidery, yet they're more challenging than simply cutting up a chicken and cooking it in a can of soup.

In my search for this compromise between frikkadels and Foie Gras, two things became very clear: the joy of creative cooking simply cannot be shrugged away, and too many shortcuts just take the heart out of everything. Be prepared, therefore, to spend a little thought and time over some dishes, but I have included little nips and tucks in most recipes in order to simplify preparation and speed things up a bit. The results should prove that it is not necessary - whether cooking for a dinner party, or simply to fill the biscuit tin – to knock oneself out in the process. Nor is it necessary to sacrifice those touches of elegance which magic the mundane into something really special.

In compiling the recipes, I have explored cuisines from all over the world, along with the latest culinary trends, but always with an eye to availability and simplicity. As always, I have used plenty of fresh vegetables and herbs; I have no time for flavour enhancers; have made little use of smoked products; and have catered for the growing trend towards substituting chicken and fish for red meat; serving salads as starters; reducing salt; and using oil instead of butter. All this, however, in moderation. This is not a wholefood book, or a guide to healthy eating. Most of the desserts are quite wanton, although fruit salads are included. The upshot is that there should be something for everyone.

Producing this book has been hard work and a huge discipline - all food writers know of that daunting, witching hour when everyone else is watching television and you're back there in the kitchen: it's time to create; your nerves are as taut as dental floss; you simmer and stir, taste, evaluate, make notes, swear; working on even a short-cut recipe takes time, and your family starts eating the curtains. Fortunately, my particular family is incredibly supportive. Month after month they have foregone their favourite foods (frikkadels?) in order to dine off a new concoction. Without them, I could not have written this book and they deserve my thanks for confirming the fact that, despite the heat in the kitchen, cooking can be a really rewarding, nice and easy pleasure.

Lynn Bedford Hall

8 STARTERS

TWO SMOKED SALMON STARTERS

Because smoked salmon is so expensive, one usually tries to pad it out a little to make it go further – either blended into a soup or a creamy pâté, or rolled up with something savoury inside. Here we have an entirely different approach, requiring just a flutter of shredded salmon to be served either on a crunchy bean salad sparked with anchovies, or marinated with cucumber and fanned with avocado. Serve these starters with rye bread.

SMOKED SALMON AND GREEN BEAN SALAD
400 g very slim green beans, trimmed and halved diagonally, or 300 g beans and 200 g button mushrooms, thinly sliced
1 large onion, sliced into thin rings
2 ml (½ tsp) dried dill tips
1 large red or yellow pepper, seeded and thinly julienned
120–160 g smoked salmon, rolled and thinly shredded
cultured sour cream
milled black pepper
lemon slices to garnish

DRESSING
100 ml (⅖ cup) sunflower or olive oil
1 x 50 g can anchovy fillets, drained and soaked in milk for 15 minutes
a few tufts of parsley
30 ml (2 tbsp) lemon juice
5 ml (1 tsp) sugar

Cook the beans, mushrooms (if using), onion and dill in a little unsalted water, in a large frying pan half-covered with a lid, until the beans are just tender and still bright green.

To make the dressing, place the oil, half the anchovy fillets, drained, parsley, lemon juice and sugar in a blender and blend until smooth.

Drain beans if necessary, but do not refresh. Place in a bowl and pour the dressing over them. Fork in the julienned pepper, cool, then cover and chill for 3–4 hours. Just before serving, toss in remaining anchovies, chopped, and arrange on individual plates.

Top with salmon, a dollop of sour cream, a dusting of pepper, place a slice of lemon on the side, and serve with fingers of buttered rye bread.
Serves 4–6.

MARINATED SMOKED SALMON AND CUCUMBER SALAD
A supremely quick, designer salad which looks, and tastes, superb.

160 g smoked salmon, sliced into thin strips
½ English cucumber, pared, seeded and finely diced
a few spring onions, chopped,
butter lettuce, avocado and sour cream with chives to garnish

DRESSING
45 ml (3 tbsp) sunflower oil
15 ml (1 tbsp) lemon juice
15 ml (1 tbsp) capers, rinsed and chopped
2 ml (½ tsp) mild Dijon mustard
2 ml (½ tsp) sugar
1 ml (¼ tsp) dried dill tips
a pinch of salt

Place salmon, cucumber and onions in a glass bowl, preferably a 20 cm pie dish, so that the ingredients can lie in the dressing. Mix ingredients for the dressing, pour over the salmon salad, toss to mix, then cover and refrigerate for 3–4 hours.

To serve, arrange a few lettuce leaves on individual serving plates. Place a large scoop of the salmon salad on one side, surround with slices of avocado, and finish the composition with sour cream mixed with chives. Pass a pepper mill and fingers of buttered brown bread.
Serves 4–5.

STARTERS

RED PEPPER TIMBALES WITH GREEN SALAD

An unusual starter in a bright bounce of colours. The red pepper moulds have a refreshing, savoury flavour and are a snap to prepare. The accompanying salad can comprise any fresh greens, tossed with a simple French dressing. Once turned out, encircle the moulds with the salad, and then top the greens with segments of avocado – their smooth, buttery flavour really ties the whole composition together. Serve with any of the savoury loaves from the chapter on breads.

500 g ripe red peppers, seeded and diced
600 ml (2⅖ cups) chicken stock
15 ml (1 tbsp) tomato paste
1 medium onion, chopped
5 ml (1 tsp) sugar
a pinch of salt
1 ml (¼ tsp) paprika
15 ml (1 tbsp) gelatine
45 ml (3 tbsp) water
200 ml (⅘ cup) cream, softly whipped

Place all the ingredients except the gelatine, water and cream in a saucepan, bring to the boil, then cover and simmer on low heat for 15 minutes or until the peppers are soft and the liquid reduced and syrupy. Cool briefly before puréeing on high speed in a blender until smooth. Pour into a bowl.
Sponge the gelatine in water, dissolve over low heat, then stir into the purée. Fold in the cream, check for extra salt or a pinch of sugar, and pour into 8 small rinsed ramekins or coffee cups. Refrigerate until set. To serve, unmould onto individual plates and surround with green salad.
Serves 8.

MARINATED MUSHROOM AND AVOCADO SALAD

Serve this lush, ever-so-easy, chilled starter with hot, fragrant toast.

DRESSING
60 ml (¼ cup) olive oil
30 ml (2 tbsp) sunflower oil
30 ml (2 tbsp) lemon juice
30 ml (2 tbsp) each finely chopped parsley and chives
2 ml (½ tsp) mustard powder
2 ml (½ tsp) chopped fresh thyme
1 ml (¼ tsp) salt
2 ml (½ tsp) sugar

SALAD
250 g small, white mushrooms, wiped and thinly sliced
a few spring onions, chopped
1 red pepper, seeded and thinly julienned
1–2 avocados, thinly segmented
milled black pepper

Whisk all the ingredients for the dressing with a fork until combined. Place mushrooms, onions and red pepper in a large, shallow glass or pottery bowl, add dressing, toss carefully until glistening, then cover and chill for 4–6 hours. Place the salad on individual salad plates, top generously with segmented avocado, and grind lashings of black pepper over it all.
Serves 6.

FRENCH BREAD TOASTS WITH THYME AND LEMON BUTTER
Cream 125 g soft butter with 5 ml (1 tsp) finely grated lemon rind, 15 ml (1 tbsp) fresh thyme leaves and 2 chopped spring onions. Toast slices of French bread lightly on one side, butter the untoasted side, and grill until melted.

10 STARTERS

STIR-FRIED CALAMARI AND VEGETABLE SALAD

A fantastic starter: tiny, tender calamari rings combined with lightly sauced vegetables, and everything conveniently prepared in advance and refrigerated to mingle and soften. Remember that calamari will only be tough if cooked for a moderate period – it should either be in and out of the pan, or slowly simmered. The former method is used here so it is important to use small calamari, available in tiny tubes. Serve with grilled Sesame and Garlic Toast – this may be assembled in advance, and is super served with most chilled starter salads.

15 ml (1 tbsp) sunflower oil
15 ml (1 tbsp) butter
400 g cleaned calamari tubes, sliced into thin rings
45 ml (3 tbsp) lemon juice
extra 60 ml (¼ cup) sunflower oil
2 leeks, thinly sliced
2 cloves garlic, crushed
200 g baby marrows, pared (optional) and julienned
1 medium red pepper, seeded and julienned
⅓ English cucumber (150 g), pared, seeded and julienned
125 g white mushrooms, wiped and thinly sliced
30 ml (2 tbsp) soy sauce
30 ml (2 tbsp) medium-dry sherry
5 ml (1 tsp) sugar

Heat oil and butter in a large frying pan. Add calamari and toss for about 3 minutes until it stiffens and turns white. Remove to a large glass dish and mix in lemon juice. Add extra oil to pan and stir-fry leeks, garlic, baby marrows, red pepper and cucumber for a few minutes until softening. Add mushrooms, soy sauce, sherry and sugar and toss just until mushrooms start to wilt and change colour – for about 1 minute. Add to calamari, toss to mix, then cool, cover and chill for at least 8 hours.

To serve, spoon into scallop shells, or onto individual small plates, surround with butter lettuce, and serve with Sesame and Garlic Toast.
Serves 4–6.

SESAME AND GARLIC TOAST
Cream 125 g soft butter with 30 ml (2 tbsp) toasted sesame seeds, 2 cloves crushed garlic and 2 chopped spring onions. Toast slices of French bread lightly on one side, spread the untoasted side with the butter, and grill until melted.

Starter salads have become one of the most popular beginnings to a meal as the idea is to whet, not wipe out, the appetite. Gone are the days of rich mousses and quiches, together with pink shrimps in avocados – and thankfully they've also taken with them grapefruit with sherry and a cherry. Many of the latest cookbooks simply go straight from soups to mains, but, to my mind, a starter salad never goes amiss. It gets the conversation going, and with the variety of fresh ingredients available, these salads need never be dull. Whizz up an imaginative dressing, serve with home-made bread, and you'll set the tone for whatever fine food is to follow.

ITALIAN MUSHROOM MOUNTAINS

This is a voluptuous starter* which, surprisingly, involves no stuffing, no cream, no butter and no frying. It may be completely assembled in advance, and because it is pretty filling, especially if served with one of the delicious savoury batter breads from the chapter on breads, you will need only one big mushroom per serving.

6 jumbo brown mushrooms (400 g)
fresh basil leaves
3 pickling onions, coarsely grated
2–3 cloves garlic, crushed
ripe, firm tomatoes
seasoning
Mozzarella or other melting cheese, sliced
60 ml (¼ cup) olive oil
dried origanum
butter lettuce or baby spinach leaves

Slice stems off mushrooms and arrange caps, flat sides up, in a large, lightly oiled baking dish. Cover each one with fresh basil leaves – you will need 3–5, depending on the size. Mix onions and garlic, and sprinkle over, dividing equally. Top with a thick slice of tomato. Sprinkle with a little salt and sugar. Cover generously with cheese. Drizzle 10 ml (2 tsp) olive oil over each, dust with origanum, and finish off with several grindings of black pepper. Cover loosely and set aside if working ahead.

Bake at 200 °C for about 25 minutes, until mushrooms have softened and released some bubbling juices, and cheese has spread and melted. Serve on individual, warmed plates and surround with lettuce or spinach leaves. Allow diners to help themselves to bread and butter. **Serves 6.**

* May also be served as a main meal for vegetarians, serving two mushrooms per person and adding a fresh green salad.

12 STARTERS

DIPS, SPREADS AND PÂTÉS

Eternally useful to snack on with drinks, or to serve in lieu of a starter before dinner. Surround them with crudités and breads, dot them around the room, and let guests do their own thing. These are just a few of the endless possibilities.

CRUDITÉS
It is vital that the vegetables are fresh, very young and prettily prepared – button mushrooms, cauliflower florets, celery sticks, baby marrow and cucumber sticks, lightly cooked asparagus spears, and julienned carrots.
  The mayonnaise may be lightened, if liked, with thick Bulgarian yoghurt or sour cream, bearing in mind that it must remain thick enough not to drip onto the carpet. Dips, spreads and pâtés should all be refrigerated before serving.

SESAME DIP
Mix 250 ml (1 cup) mayonnaise with 5 ml (1 tsp) soy sauce, 2 ml (½ tsp) dark sesame oil and 30 ml (2 tbsp) toasted sesame seeds.

MUSTARD AND GARLIC DIP
Mix 250 ml (1 cup) mayonnaise with 2–3 cloves garlic crushed with a little salt, 25 ml (5 tsp) wholegrain mustard, 30 ml (2 tbsp) each chopped chives and parsley, and 5 ml (1 tsp) honey.

CHILLI AND CUMIN DIP
Mix 250 ml (1 cup) mayonnaise with 1 ml (¼ tsp) chilli powder, 5 ml (1 tsp) ground cumin and 5 ml (1 tsp) tomato paste.

SMOKED SALMON DIP
Mix 125 g chopped smoked salmon, 250 g smooth, low-fat cottage cheese, 15 ml (1 tbsp) gin, 2 chopped spring onions, 30 ml (2 tbsp) sour cream, a pinch of sugar, a dash of lemon juice and a grind of black pepper.

ANCHOVY AND GREEN PEPPER DIP
Drain 1 x 50 g can anchovies and soak in milk for 10 minutes to reduce saltiness. Drain and place in a processor fitted with the metal blade, together with 250 ml (60 g) white breadcrumbs, 1 small green pepper, seeded and diced, and 2 spring onions, chopped. Process until well blended. Add 45 ml (3 tbsp) each cultured sour cream and mayonnaise and process again, then add a little lemon juice to taste.

FRESH HERB DIP
Mix 125 ml (½ cup) each mayonnaise and sour cream, 60 ml (4 tbsp) each chopped parsley and basil leaves, 2 chopped spring onions, and salt, black pepper and fresh lemon juice to taste.

MUSHROOM AND CREAM CHEESE PÂTÉ
30 ml (2 tbsp) each sunflower oil and butter
60 ml (¼ cup) sweet sherry
15 ml (1 tbsp) soy sauce
5 ml (1 tsp) chopped rosemary leaves
2 cloves garlic, crushed
1 smallish onion, chopped
250 g white mushrooms, wiped and finely chopped
250 g cream cheese or low-fat cottage cheese
60 ml (4 tbsp) chopped parsley
30 ml (2 tbsp) chopped chives
a pinch of sugar

Heat oil, butter, sherry, soy sauce, rosemary, garlic and onion. Add mushrooms and sauté until soft and liquid absorbed, but still very moist. Remove from stove, slowly stir in cheese, add herbs and sugar, then pot and chill.
Makes 500 ml (2 cups).

STARTERS 13

QUICK HUMMUS
Hummus is a totally addictive Middle Eastern purée, based on chickpeas and served with pita breads and salads, or as a dip with vegetables. Although the flavour of freshly cooked chickpeas cannot be matched, they do require a lengthy soaking and cooking period. Using the canned product makes it possible to whizz up a tasty hummus in minutes.

1 x 425 g can chickpeas, drained and liquid reserved
45 ml (3 tbsp) tahini*
15 ml (1 tbsp) olive oil
1 clove garlic, chopped
30 ml (2 tbsp) lemon juice
2 ml (½ tsp) ground cumin
salt and white pepper to taste
olive oil, toasted sesame seeds and finely chopped parsley to garnish

Slip the skins off the chickpeas and discard. Place all the ingredients in a processor fitted with the metal blade and grind to a pulp. Slowly, while processing, pour in enough of the reserved liquid to make a smooth and creamy purée. You will have to stop and scrape down the sides a few times, and finish off on high speed. Turn into a pottery bowl and chill for several hours.
  Before serving, drizzle a little olive oil over the top, sprinkle generously with sesame seeds, and finish with a flurry of parsley.
Makes about 400 ml (1⅗ cup).

* Tahini is a sesame seed paste available from health shops or speciality stores.

VARIATION
Instead of chickpeas, use 1 x 410 g can butter beans. Drain and discard the liquid, using 45 ml (3 tbsp) water instead of the reserved chickpea liquid when processing.
Makes about 350 ml (1⅖ cup).

CHUNKY CHICKEN LIVER AND MUSHROOM PÂTÉ
Another recipe for the ubiquitous old favourite – but this one is possibly a little different from the one you've been making for years.

250 g chicken livers
15 ml (1 tbsp) sunflower oil
60 g butter
1 medium onion, finely chopped
1 ml (¼ tsp) dried thyme
125 g white mushrooms, wiped and diced
30 ml (2 tbsp) sweet sherry
15 ml (1 tbsp) soy sauce
1 ml (¼ tsp) grated nutmeg
2 ml (½ tsp) gelatine
60 ml (¼ cup) beef stock

Rinse livers in vinegar-water, pat dry and halve, discarding any green bits. Heat the oil and half the butter in a pan and fry onions until well browned – adding a pinch of sugar helps the process. Reduce heat and add livers and thyme. Toss for a few minutes, until livers are browned and the aroma is inviting – whether you leave them a little pink inside or browned right through is a matter of choice – but do not overcook. Remove pan from stove and, when contents are no longer steaming, transfer to a food processor fitted with the metal blade and process until smooth.
  Heat remaining butter in a clean pan, add mushrooms, and, when softening, add sherry, soy sauce and nutmeg. Allow to bubble up, then remove from stove and cool slightly before adding to livers. Process in quick pulses to mix, without mashing the mushrooms. Spoon into a shallow pottery bowl and cool.
  Sponge gelatine in stock, dissolve over low heat, allow to cool but not to gel, then pour slowly over cold pâté to cover surface thinly. Chill for several hours or preferably overnight.
Makes 375 ml (1½ cups).

APPLE AND CELERY VICHYSSOISE

A mellow, golden soup with an intriguing flavour. Easy to make, the ingredients are basic, and it may be served hot or cold.

15 ml (1 tbsp) each sunflower oil and butter
1 medium onion, chopped
2 leeks, chopped
5 ml (1 tsp) each curry powder and ground ginger
2 medium potatoes (about 300 g), peeled and cubed
2 Golden Delicious apples (about 225 g), peeled and cubed
3 large sticks table celery, plus some leaves, chopped
1 litre (4 cups) chicken stock
2 ml (½ tsp) salt
2 bay leaves
125–250 ml (½–1 cup) cream
small celery leaves or a flutter of freshly grated apple to garnish

Heat oil and butter in a large saucepan, add onion, leeks and spices, and toss together to cook spices and soften vegetables – keep heat low as they should not brown. Add potatoes, apples and celery, and stir until mixed and aromatic. Add remaining ingredients except cream, then cover and simmer gently for about 20 minutes, until vegetables and apples are soft.

Cool until no longer steaming, remove bay leaves, and purée in a blender, in batches, until smooth. Return to saucepan and stir in cream – use enough to enrich and thin soup to the desired consistency. Check for salt and possibly a little sugar, and reheat without boiling, garnish and serve, or, if preferred, do not reheat, just refrigerate, and then serve cold.
Serves 5–6.

CHILLED CUCUMBER, AVOCADO AND YOGHURT SOUP

A no-cook, summery soup in palest peppermint-green. Although rich and creamy in appearance, the flavour is refreshingly tangy. Don't skip the walnuts – they add a nice fillip to the otherwise chaste ingredients. For extra flavour, toast lightly before crushing.

500 g English cucumber
2 spring onions, chopped
½ large avocado, diced
10 ml (2 tsp) lemon juice
½ small clove garlic
500 ml (2 cups) low-fat, stirred Bulgarian yoghurt*
a little salt and a big pinch of sugar
2 sprigs of mint
coarsely crushed walnuts and milled black pepper to garnish

It is important to use the correct weight of cucumber – 500 g is about three-quarters of one cucumber. Peel, seed and dice, then spread on a plate, sprinkle with salt, and leave to stand for 30 minutes. Rinse well in a colander and shake dry. Place in a blender with onions, avocado, lemon juice, garlic and yoghurt, and blend until smooth.

Pour into a fridge container, add salt, sugar and unchopped mint, cover, and refrigerate for 4–6 hours. The colour and flavour will hold overnight, but yoghurt tends to become sharper in taste the longer it stands.

Remove mint before serving, and pour into chilled bowls. Grind a little pepper on top of each serving, and sprinkle 1 tsp walnuts in the centre.
Serves 4–6.

* Stirred Bulgarian yoghurt is a liquid, pouring yoghurt and is the one to use here – not thick, set Bulgarian yoghurt.

QUICK GAZPACHO WITH WHIPPED BASIL CREAM

This is a really speedy version of the popular Spanish summer soup, using a method which, although not traditional, puts it within reach of the busiest cook. Normally gazpacho is served with chopped salad goodies and croûtons, but a surprising topping of savoury cream gives this old favourite a new look and flavour.

2 x 2 cm slices crustless bread
600 g ripe tomatoes, peeled, seeded and chopped
1 large English cucumber, peeled, seeded and chopped
1 clove garlic
1 large leek, chopped (white part only)
400 ml (1 $\frac{3}{5}$ cups) tomato juice (not tomato cocktail)
5 ml (1 tsp) each salt and sugar
15 ml (1 tbsp) red wine vinegar
30 ml (2 tbsp) olive oil
1 red pepper, seeded and chopped

BASIL CREAM
125 ml ($\frac{1}{2}$ cup) cream
10 basil leaves, chopped
a pinch of salt and a little black pepper

Soak bread briefly in a little water and squeeze dry, then mix with remaining ingredients in a large bowl. Spoon into a blender and purée in batches, until smooth. Do not expect a velvety result – although the vegetables should be completely pulped, the mixture will appear mushy and rather thick. This is correct, as gazpacho is served over ice cubes, which thin it down a little. Turn into a fridge container and chill. Gazpacho should be served after about 2 hours in the refrigerator, but will hold overnight.

Make cream by whisking all ingredients together until thick. Chill until required. Give the soup a good stir before serving, and check seasoning. Pour into chilled bowls over a cube or two of ice, and top each serving with a dollop of cream.
Serves 8.

VARIATION
Omit bread and blend vegetables very briefly, leaving them chunky. Without the substance of the bread, this is rather like a drinkable salad.

FRENCH ONION SOUP

Originally a soup for the working classes in Paris, this thick broth should be made with genuine meat stock, which takes about 5 hours to prepare. Understandably, we cheat in this regard, but one step that should never be short-changed is browning the onions.

45 ml (3 tbsp) butter
30 ml (2 tbsp) sunflower oil
500 g onions, peeled and sliced into thin rings*
5 ml (1 tsp) sugar
15 ml (1 tbsp) flour
1,25 litres (5 cups) hot beef stock (cubes will have to do)
15 ml (1 tbsp) brandy
2 bay leaves
6 slices French bread
60 g grated cheese – choose from Gruyère, Parmesan or Cheddar, or a mixture
5 ml (1 tsp) each Dijon mustard and butter

Heat butter and oil in a heavy-based saucepan, add onions and sugar (this is optional but helps them to caramelise), and cook very slowly over low heat, tossing occasionally, until very well browned. This should take at least 10 minutes, and care must be taken that they do not scorch. Sprinkle in flour, then slowly stir in stock. Add brandy and bay leaves, cover and simmer gently for 20–30 minutes. Cool.

Toast bread on one side. Mash cheese to a paste with mustard and butter, and spread on untoasted side. This may be done in advance. Remove bay leaves from soup, check seasoning and reheat. Place bread under grill until cheese melts. Place one slice in the bottom of each smallish, deep, heated soup bowl, and ladle hot soup over the top.
Serves 6.

* Chill onions before slicing for fewer tears.

LISA'S SOUP

A thick, chunky soup, which I have been making on winter week-ends for years. My daughter insisted I include it in this book, but I found it difficult to come up with exact quantities as it's a kindly soup that will accept almost anything you have in reach. These are the basics.

30 ml (2 tbsp) sunflower oil
15 ml (1 tbsp) butter
1 large onion, chopped
1 clove garlic, crushed
5 ml (1 tsp) sugar
300 g frozen mixed vegetables
2 ml (½ tsp) dried thyme
1,5 litres (6 cups) beef stock
a handful of chopped parsley
2 bay leaves
45 ml (3 tbsp) tomato paste
250 ml (180 g) soup mixture, rinsed
2 ml (½ tsp) salt

Heat oil and butter, add onion, garlic and sugar, stir until lightly browned, then add vegetables and thyme. Toss until hot, add remaining ingredients, bring to boil, reduce heat and simmer gently for about 30 minutes, stirring now and then. Check seasoning. This soup reheats well, and loves a smidgin of pesto.
Serves 5–6.

QUICK CHILLED PEA SOUP
500 g frozen peas
1 litre (4 cups) chicken stock
2 pickling onions, chopped
2 apples, peeled and chopped
24 large mint leaves
a few tufts of parsley
2 ml (½ tsp) each salt and sugar
thick, chilled cream
a little sherry

Slowly bring all ingredients except cream and sherry to boil, cover and simmer until soft. Cool, then purée in batches in blender. Refrigerate. Add cream and sherry to taste, then serve.

EMERALD SUMMER SOUP

Combine avocados with spinach and you get a soup with a sensational colour. It is more or less instant to make, velvety in texture, and refreshingly pure in flavour – but remember when planning the menu that avocado soups are rich, and this one is no exception.

90 g (2 cups) shredded spinach leaves, firmly packed for measuring
a few tufts of parsley
1 extra-large avocado, peeled and diced
2 slim spring onions, plus some green tops, chopped
500 ml (2 cups) warm chicken stock
15 ml (1 tbsp) lemon juice
125 ml (½ cup) thin cream
a pinch each of salt, white pepper and sugar
wafer-thin slices of avocado to garnish

Pour boiling water over the spinach and parsley, stand for a few minutes until wilted, then drain. Place all the ingredients in a blender and blend until smooth. The spinach probably will not disappear entirely, but should be reduced to minute little flecks. Pour into a glass jar and close. Chill well. It will keep overnight, although the colour will fade a little.

Stir well before serving, check seasoning, and, if too thick, thin down with a little extra cream or milk. Spoon the soup into chilled bowls – white china will highlight the colour beautifully – and garnish with wafers of avocado.
Serves 6.

QUICK LOW-KILOJOULE ORIENTAL MUSHROOM SOUP

This pure and simple recipe shows just what can be done with a jug of stock and some fresh vegetables. The flavour is great, but the colour is funky-dark so be sure to garnish this one cheerfully.

30 ml (2 tbsp) sunflower oil
2 leeks, thinly sliced
5 ml (1 tsp) chopped, peeled root ginger
250 g brown mushrooms, wiped and chopped
2 sticks table celery, plus some leaves, chopped
2–3 carrots, cut into small, thin matchsticks
4–6 spinach leaves, shredded
1,25 litres (5 cups) beef stock
30 ml (2 tbsp) medium-dry sherry
10 ml (2 tsp) soy sauce
a pinch of sugar
45 g vermicelli, broken, or rice noodles
slivers of carrots, leeks or spring onions, crisped in iced water, to garnish

Heat the oil in a large saucepan and lightly fry the leeks and ginger. Reduce the heat, add all the vegetables, and toss until limp and shiny.

Add the remaining ingredients, bring to the boil, then cover with a lid and simmer gently for about 10 minutes. Ladle into Chinese soup bowls and garnish with carrots, leeks or spring onions.
Serves 6.

BABY MARROW AND MELTED BRIE SOUP

A whiff of Brie cheese gives a basic vegetable soup an elusive flavour and a creamy texture. A touch of dill adds further interest to this rich, special-occasion soup. Most of the preparation may be done in advance.

60 ml (¼ cup) sunflower oil
a small nut of butter
4 leeks, sliced
2 medium onions, chopped
250 g potatoes, peeled and cubed
5 ml (1 tsp) dried dill tips
600 g baby marrows, pared and sliced
1,25 litres (5 cups) chicken stock
5 ml (1 tsp) salt
125 g Brie cheese
125 ml (½ cup) milk or thin cream
snipped chives to garnish

Place oil, butter, leeks, onions, potatoes, dill and baby marrows in a large saucepan and sweat over low heat, shaking pan occasionally, until softening. Add stock and salt, cover and simmer until vegetables are cooked. Cool slightly, then purée in a blender until smooth. If too thick, add a little extra stock. If working ahead, stop here.

Remove rind from cheese and discard, then cube the creamy inside. Return purée to saucepan and reheat on low heat, adding cheese and milk or cream. Stir until cheese has melted and soup is piping hot. Check seasoning – you will probably need a little milled black pepper. Spoon into heated bowls and garnish.
Serves 8.

A flutter of fresh herbs can transform a bowl of soup. Grow some right outside your kitchen for ease and convenience.

SPEEDY SPINACH SOUP

Using frozen spinach cuts down on time when making this light, silky soup. Touches of nutmeg and port add an elusive flavour, and a sprinkling of feta lifts the intense green colour.

15 ml (1 tbsp) each sunflower oil and butter
1 large onion, chopped
2 leeks, sliced
300 g potatoes, peeled and cubed
625 ml (2½ cups) chicken stock
a little salt and a pinch of sugar
2 bay leaves
a few tufts of parsley
1 x 250 g packet frozen spinach, thawed
1 ml (¼ tsp) grated nutmeg
250 ml (1 cup) milk
25 ml (5 tsp) port
feta cheese to garnish

Heat oil and butter. Add onion and leeks, and soften without browning. Add potatoes, toss to mix, then add stock, seasoning, bay leaves and parsley.

Cover and simmer gently for 15 minutes. Add spinach and nutmeg and simmer for a further 5 minutes.

Cool slightly, remove bay leaves, add milk, and purée in a blender, in batches, until smooth. Return to the saucepan, add port, and reheat gently. Check seasoning and, if soup needs thinning, stir in extra milk or cream. Ladle into heated bowls and sprinkle with feta.
Serves 6.

SOUPS 19

GRANNY'S BEEF AND BARLEY BROTH

Memories are made of this kind of homely fare.

2 slices beef shin with marrow bone (about 300 g)
30 ml (2 tbsp) each sunflower oil and butter
2 large onions, chopped
4–6 carrots, diced
250 ml (180 g) pearl barley, rinsed
125 ml (90 g) red lentils, rinsed
3 litres (12 cups) water
200 ml (4/5 cup) tomato purée
1 large potato, peeled and coarsely grated
2 bay leaves
a handful of chopped parsley
2 ml (½ tsp) dried thyme, crushed
10 ml (2 tsp) salt
5 ml (1 tsp) sugar
shredded spinach
extra chopped parsley to garnish

Do not slice shin, but nick the edges to prevent curling. Heat oil and butter in a large, heavy saucepan and brown shin on both sides. Remove and set aside. Add onions to pan and fry until browned – adding a pinch of sugar will enhance the colour.

Reduce heat, return meat to the pan, and add remaining ingredients except spinach. Stir to mix, then cover and simmer on very low heat for 1½ hours, stirring occasionally and adding a little more water if the soup becomes too thick.

Remove meat and shred, discarding bones and any sinew. Return to soup and add a handful or two of spinach. Reheat, stirring, until spinach has wilted, then remove bay leaves, check seasoning, pour into a large tureen, and sprinkle with chopped parsley.
Serves 8–10.

AROMATIC DHAL SOUP

An ochre-coloured, spicy soup. Sure to tempt diners who enjoy exotic flavours, and incredibly easy and economical.

30 ml (2 tbsp) each sunflower oil and butter
2 medium onions, chopped
3 cloves garlic, crushed
2 sticks cinnamon
5 ml (1 tsp) each ground cumin and garam masala
10 ml (2 tsp) each ground coriander and turmeric
500 ml (360 g) red lentils, rinsed
2 litres (8 cups) chicken stock
a little salt
5 ml (1 tsp) sugar
30 ml (2 tbsp) tomato paste
1 medium (125 g) potato, peeled and coarsely grated
thick Bulgarian yoghurt and chopped fresh coriander to garnish*

Heat oil and butter in a large saucepan. Add onions and garlic and, when softening, add spices. Allow them to sizzle for a minute or two on low heat, adding a dash of water if necessary to prevent scorching.

Add remaining ingredients, bring to the boil, then cover and simmer gently, stirring occasionally, for about 25 minutes or until lentils and potato are soft and the ingredients have cooked almost to a purée. Stir vigorously to combine and, if too thick, add a little more stock. Check seasoning, remove cinnamon, and serve in heated bowls. Top each serving with a teaspoon of yoghurt and sprinkle with chopped coriander.
Serves 8–10.

* Use a mere flutter of coriander leaves as their rather dominant flavour could mask the flavour of the soup; if unavailable, use fresh mint, parsley or chives.

BAKED SESAME FISH

Elegant fish in a feather-light sauce. The flavour is subtly exotic, and, best of all, the entire dish is assembled in minutes and most of the cooking takes place in the oven. This fish is saucy enough to serve with rice, and stir-fried vegetables make a fitting accompaniment.

600–700 g fish fillets, skinned (kabeljou is a prime choice)
seasoned flour
250 ml (1 cup) fish or chicken stock
25 ml (5 tsp) soy sauce
15 ml (1 tbsp) butter
4 spring onions, chopped
5 ml (1 tsp) finely chopped, peeled root ginger
15 ml (1 tbsp) lemon juice
5 ml (1 tsp) honey
5 ml (1 tsp) dark sesame oil
15 ml (1 tbsp) cornflour
30 ml (2 tbsp) sweet sherry
toasted sesame seeds

Slice fish into 4 equal pieces, or leave in 2 large fillets. Roll in seasoned flour and place in a buttered baking dish to lie flat without overlapping.
  Mix stock, soy sauce, butter, onions, ginger, lemon juice, honey, sesame oil and cornflour in a small saucepan and bring to the boil, stirring. When thickened, stir in the sherry, and pour over the fish. Sprinkle generously with sesame seeds and bake, uncovered, at 180 °C for about 30 minutes, or until the sauce is bubbling and the fish cooked through.
Serves 4.

HINT
If you can lay your hands on some lemon grass, add a few stalks when making the sauce (use the white or pale part of the stem). Remove before serving – the delicate flavour will linger deliciously.

FISH AND SEAFOOD

FISH WITH STIR-FRIED VEGETABLES

This is light, and the flavours are finely attuned. Serve with rice.

45 ml (3 tbsp) sunflower oil
5 ml (1 tsp) dark sesame oil
1 onion, sliced into thin rings
5 ml (1 tsp) chopped, peeled root ginger
3 medium carrots, julienned
180 g slender green beans, trimmed and sliced
½ English cucumber, pared and julienned
125 g white mushrooms, wiped and sliced
600 g white fish steaks, skinned and deboned
salt and pepper
toasted almonds to garnish

SAUCE
250 ml (1 cup) fish or chicken stock
15 ml (1 tbsp) cornflour
15 ml (1 tbsp) soy sauce
5 ml (1 tsp) honey
2 ml (½ tsp) finely grated lemon rind

Heat oils in a large frying pan and stir-fry onion, ginger, carrots and beans until softening but still crunchy. Add cucumber and mushrooms and, keeping heat fairly low, toss until just wilting. Stir together all ingredients for the sauce and add to the pan. When bubbling and thickened, reduce heat to very low and arrange lightly seasoned fish on top of vegetables. Cover and allow to simmer very gently for 10–12 minutes or until fish just flakes. Using a slotted spoon, transfer fish to a warmed serving platter and spoon vegetables and sauce over top.* Sprinkle with almonds and serve immediately.
Serves 4.

* If the fish adds juices to the sauce, leave the sauce in the pan and reduce over high heat, then pour over the assembled dish.

FISH BAKED WITH TOMATOES AND BASIL BUTTER

An unpretentious but jolly pleasing fish dish which highlights the blissful friendship between basil, tomatoes and Parmesan cheese. Use a firm, non-oily fish – even hake will do as long as it's fresh – and affirm the Italian image by serving with pasta and creamed spinach.

1 large onion, sliced into thin rings
250 g tomatoes, sliced into rings
seasoning
60 ml (¼ cup) off-dry white wine
600 g fish fillets, skinned and cut into 2 large or 4 smaller pieces
seasoned flour
60 g butter
2 cloves garlic, crushed
2 ml (½ tsp) finely grated lemon rind
8–10 large basil leaves, chopped
ground black pepper
grated cheese – either Parmesan or a mixture of Parmesan and Cheddar
a few basil leaves to garnish

Brush the base of a medium-sized baking dish with olive or sunflower oil, cover with onion rings and top with tomato slices. Sprinkle with salt and a pinch of sugar and pour in the wine. If you are working ahead, set aside at this stage.
  Just before baking, dust fish with seasoned flour and place in a single layer on top of the tomatoes.
  Melt butter with garlic, lemon rind, basil and pepper, pour over fish, sprinkle with the grated cheese, and bake, uncovered, at 180 °C for about 25 minutes, until bubbling and succulent and fish is cooked through. Garnish with basil.
Serves 4.

EXTRA EASY LOW-KILOJOULE FISH DISH

Tailor this one to suit your needs. You could edge overboard by stirring a little cream into the sauce right at the end, and topping the dish with a sprinkling of toasted almonds. Then again, you could keep it pure and serve it just as it is, with a green salad – spinach and sprouts would be good – and rice tossed with lightly sautéed mushrooms.

4 white fish fillets (about 700 g), skinned
125 ml (½ cup) fresh orange juice
1 ml (¼ tsp) very finely grated orange rind
5 ml (1 tsp) chopped, peeled root ginger
15 ml (1 tbsp) oyster sauce
10 ml (2 tsp) soy sauce
6 spring onions, chopped
100 ml (⅖ cup) off-dry white wine
15 ml (1 tbsp) sunflower oil
5 ml (1 tsp) honey
extra 50 ml (⅕ cup) orange juice
extra 5 ml (1 tsp) soy sauce
10 ml (2 tsp) cornflour
chopped fresh fennel or snipped chives to garnish

Place fillets, without overlapping, in a flattish glass bowl. Mix orange juice, rind, ginger, oyster sauce, soy sauce, onions, wine, oil and honey. Pour over fish and marinate in refrigerator for 2 hours, turning once.

Place fish and marinade in a large frying pan, bring to the boil, then reduce heat and simmer, covered, for about 5 minutes or until fish is just cooked.

Using a slotted spoon, remove to serving platter and keep warm. Mix extra orange juice, soy sauce and cornflour, add to pan juices and boil up, stirring, until thickened. Pour over fish, garnish and serve.
Serves 4.

SIMPLE FISH CURRY

This is a yeoman dish, totally without pretensions. Low in fat and low in cost, it makes a nourishing and satisfying family meal.

30 ml (2 tbsp) sunflower oil
1 large onion, chopped
2 cloves garlic, crushed
15 ml (1 tbsp) curry powder
5 ml (1 tsp) peeled, chopped root ginger
2 ml (½ tsp) turmeric
2 star anise
125 ml (½ cup) fish or chicken stock
1 x 400 g can tomatoes, chopped, plus juice
2 bay leaves
a pinch of salt
5 ml (1 tsp) sugar
30 ml (2 tbsp) chutney
600 g white fish fillets, skinned
seasoned flour
coriander leaves or chopped parsley to garnish

Heat oil, add onion, and, when softened, add garlic and all the spices. Stir on low heat for 1–2 minutes, then add stock, tomatoes, bay leaves, salt, sugar and chutney. Bring to the boil, stirring, then simmer very gently, uncovered, for about 10 minutes to thicken slightly and concentrate the flavour.

Meanwhile, roll fish in seasoned flour and arrange in a buttered baking dish to fit. Pour sauce over the top – it should cover the fish completely.

Bake, uncovered, at 180 °C for 25–30 minutes or until the fish flakes when tested with a fork – the exact time depends on whether the fish is fresh or cooked from frozen. Remove bay leaves and anise, and garnish.
Serves 4.

FISH AND SEAFOOD 23

SPICED FISH IN CHILLI-TOMATO SAUCE

A flamboyantly coloured dish with a nice bite and lots of character. It is very easy to cook as, once spiced, the fish is simply slid into the bright, bubbling sauce and left to simmer and absorb the flavours. Serve with Basmati rice, or see the note at the end of the recipe for my favourite, easy alternative.

30 ml (2 tbsp) sunflower oil
2 ml (½ tsp) ground ginger
5 ml (1 tsp) each ground cumin and coriander
2 cloves garlic, crushed
2 ml (½ tsp) salt
4 white fish fillets (600 g), skinned*
1 x 400 g can tomatoes, finely chopped, plus juice
1 medium onion, finely chopped
1 each fresh red and green chilli, seeded and chopped
1 green pepper, seeded and chopped
a little salt
5 ml (1 tsp) sugar
60 ml (¼ cup) water
30 ml (2 tbsp) chutney
chopped parsley or coriander leaves to garnish

Mix oil with spices, garlic and salt, brush onto both sides of fish, and refrigerate for at least 2 hours. Mix the remaining ingredients in a large frying pan, bring to the boil, stirring, then reduce heat and simmer, covered, for 10 minutes.

Slide in fish, spoon sauce over it, then cover and simmer for about 10 minutes or until cooked. Using a slotted spoon, transfer fish to a heated serving dish and keep warm.

Boil sauce over high heat for a few minutes, until slightly reduced and thickened, pour over fish, garnish and serve. **Serves 4.**

* You can use budget hake or stylish kingklip with equal success, as long as they are fresh.

NOTE
Use 250 ml (200 g) long-grain, white rice and add 3 bay leaves, 2 star anise, 2 ml (½ tsp) ground fennel and 2 whole cloves before bringing to the boil. Once cooked, add a lump of butter.

24 FISH AND SEAFOOD

FISH BAKED IN A CHUNKY MUSHROOM SAUCE

This dish does not pretend to be anything but plain useful and quick, nevertheless it is ideal for home cooks faced with having to produce a meal at the end of one of THOSE days. The ingredients are minimal, and the fish comes straight from the freezer. The only item for which you will probably have to step out of the kitchen is the garnish, but, as always, fresh herbs make such a difference to both appearance and flavour.

**600 g frozen fillets of hake
30 ml (2 tbsp) flour mixed with 2 ml (½ tsp) salt
150 g white mushrooms, wiped and thinly sliced
175 ml (⅔ cup) cultured sour cream
15 ml (1 tbsp) Dijon mustard
30 ml (2 tbsp) brandy
6 spring onions, chopped
chopped fresh dill and/or fennel**

Remove skin from fish – it is easily pulled off while frozen, using a sharp knife and starting at the thin, tail end of the fillet. Roll fish in the seasoned flour, coating well, and arrange in a well-buttered baking dish to fit closely without overlapping. Sprinkle any remaining seasoned flour over the top.

Mix remaining ingredients except herbs, and spread over to cover each fillet completely – the mixture will be thick, but the mushrooms and fish will release juices while baking.

Bake, uncovered, at 180 °C for 30–35 minutes, until the fish is cooked through. Sprinkle generously with the chopped dill and/or fennel, and serve at once.
Serves 4.

ALMOND KINGKLIP WITH PERNOD AND PARSLEY BUTTER

Kingklip is a genteel fish that needs to be treated simply but with style and the following recipe combines these requirements really well. For this dish it is essential to use long, thin, tail-end fillets rather than thick loin portions. The same applies to any other fish you might prefer to use.

**6 thin kingklip fillets (about 200 g each), skinned
seasoned flour
toasted, slivered almonds**

FLAVOURED BUTTER
**125 g soft butter
15 ml (1 tbsp) Pernod
a large pinch of dried dill*
30 ml (2 tbsp) very finely chopped parsley**

First make flavoured butter: beat butter until creamy, then slowly beat in Pernod, dill and parsley. Taste a smidgin – you might want more dill. Shape into a roll, wrap, and chill or freeze until firm enough to slice.

Dust fish with seasoned flour, shake off excess, and arrange in a shallow baking dish to fit. Slice butter and arrange small pats along the length of each fillet.

Bake, uncovered, at 180 °C for 15 minutes. Sprinkle with almonds and bake for another 5 minutes, or until the fish is just cooked through. Serve immediately, with the buttery juices spooned over.
Serves 6.

* Dried dill has been used for the sake of convenience because the fresh herb is not always available. If substituting fresh dill, use more – dried dill is strongly flavoured and should be used in small quantities.

FISH AND SEAFOOD 25

CALAMARI AND MUSHROOM GOULASH

A deliciously voluptuous stew.

60 ml (¼ cup) sunflower oil
a nut of butter
1 large onion, finely chopped
1 red pepper, seeded and diced
800 g cleaned calamari tubes, sliced into thin rings
400 g white mushrooms, wiped and sliced
15 ml (1 tbsp) flour
10 ml (2 tsp) paprika
600 g juicy tomatoes, skinned and chopped
30 ml (2 tbsp) tomato paste
5 ml (1 tsp) salt
10 ml (2 tsp) sugar
125 ml (½ cup) red wine
2 cloves garlic, crushed
2 bay leaves
45 ml (3 tbsp) chopped fresh basil leaves (not dried)
60 ml (¼ cup) cultured sour cream

Heat oil and butter in a very large, heavy frying pan or saucepan. Add onion and red pepper and, when softening, add calamari. Toss for a few minutes, until it stiffens and turns white, then reduce heat to very low.

Add mushrooms and, when softening, sprinkle in flour and paprika and stir until absorbed. Add remaining ingredients except basil and cream, stir, cover and simmer *very gently*, for about 50 minutes, stirring occasionally.

Initially the mixture will be very thick, but the calamari and mushrooms will gradually release their moisture; you will, however, need to add a little stock or water during the cooking period. When the goulash is ready, the calamari should be very tender in a bright, thickish sauce.

Remove bay leaves, check seasoning, swirl in the basil and cream, and serve with pasta. Serves 6.

SALMON CUTLETS WITH AN ITALIAN-STYLE SAUCE

The quickest way of serving fish is with a pat of savoury butter; second in line is to stir up a sauce while the fish is baking. The following is an unusually robust sauce to serve with fish, but the pesto mellows it perfectly and adds an engaging Mediterranean flavour. Serve with buttered noodles, or creamed potatoes and a spinach salad.

15 ml (1 tbsp) each olive oil and butter
1 medium onion, finely chopped
1 clove garlic, crushed
125 g white mushrooms, wiped and sliced
1 x 400 g can tomatoes (ready chopped are best)
15 ml (1 tbsp) capers, rinsed and chopped
5 ml (1 tsp) sugar
a little salt
60 ml (4 tbsp) chopped parsley
4 salmon cutlets (about 600 g)
melted butter to brush over fish
15 ml (1 tbsp) pesto

Heat oil and butter, add onion, garlic and mushrooms, stir until softening, then add remaining ingredients except fish and pesto, and simmer on low heat, uncovered, for about 8 minutes, stirring occasionally, until thickened and reduced.

Meanwhile, season fish, brush with melted butter, and bake or grill until cooked. Stir pesto into sauce, place fish on a heated serving platter, and spoon sauce over or alongside the fish.
Serves 4.

FISH WITH MUSTARD AND CAPER CREAM SAUCE

Use perfectly shaped, medium-thick fillets for this fuss-free fish, napped with a sauce elegantly flavoured with simple ingredients.

125 ml (½ cup) water
60 ml (¼ cup) white wine
2 ml (½ tsp) salt
1 pickling onion, chopped
4 white fish fillets (about 500 g), skinned

SAUCE
30 ml (2 tbsp) butter
30 ml (2 tbsp) flour
125 ml (½ cup) reserved poaching liquid
125 ml (½ cup) cream
15 ml (1 tbsp) Dijon mustard
10 ml (2 tsp) capers, rinsed and chopped
15 ml (1 tbsp) chopped chives

Bring water, wine, salt and onion to the boil in a large frying pan. Add fish, immediately reduce heat and simmer, covered, until fish is just cooked – this should take only a few minutes.

Using a slotted spoon, transfer fish to a lightly oiled baking dish to fit closely without crowding. Strain the poaching liquid and reserve.

Make the sauce by melting butter in a small saucepan. Stir in flour and, when absorbed and straw-coloured, slowly stir in fish stock and cream, then add remaining ingredients. When thickened and bubbling, pour over fish and quickly heat through in oven at 180 °C. Good partners are a succulent mushroom rice and a crisp and fresh green salad.
Serves 4.

SAUCY BAKED FISH WITH CRUMB TOPPING

This is fast fish at its succulent best, with a wonderful waft of Italian flavours. Neither thawed nor fried, the fillets are simply covered with a tomato-vegetable sauce, topped with garlicky Parmesan crumbs, and baked. The result is a prime example of how easy it is to perk up basic, inexpensive ingredients.

600 g frozen, skinned and deboned whiting fillets
salt and pepper

SAUCE
30 ml (2 tbsp) olive or sunflower oil
1 large onion, finely chopped
250 g baby marrows, pared and sliced
1 stick table celery, chopped
500 g ripe tomatoes, skinned and chopped*
a handful of chopped parsley
60 ml (¼ cup) dry vermouth
5 ml (1 tsp) each salt and sugar
2 ml (½ tsp) dried tarragon

CRUMB TOPPING
30 ml (2 tbsp) butter
2–3 cloves garlic, crushed
300 ml (75 g) white or brown breadcrumbs
30 ml (2 tbsp) grated Parmesan cheese

First make sauce: heat oil and sauté onion. Add marrows and celery and toss briefly. Add remaining ingredients for sauce, stir to mix, then cover and simmer on very low heat for about 25 minutes, stirring occasionally. When done, the mixture should be moist but not watery – the fish will add a little juice. Set the sauce aside while making the topping.

To make the topping, melt butter with garlic, add crumbs, and toss until butter is absorbed. Remove from stove, mix in Parmesan, and set aside.

FISH AND SEAFOOD

Arrange the frozen fillets in a buttered baking dish to fit without overlapping. Season lightly, cover with the vegetable sauce, sprinkle with the topping, and bake, uncovered, at 180 °C for 30–35 minutes or until the sauce is bubbling and the fish is cooked through.
Serves 4 generously.

* Do use fresh rather than canned tomatoes for this sauce.

FISH WITH ALMOND AND FENNEL BUTTER SAUCE

A swirl of browned butter with nuts and herbs adds a gourmet touch to almost any kind of fish. This is not a sauce to be made in advance, but that isn't a bother as it is so quickly mustered. If finding fresh fennel is a problem, leave it out, as long as you stick with the other herbs.

4 fish fillets (about 600 g), skinned
60 g butter
45–60 g almond strips
30 ml (2 tbsp) lemon juice
30 ml (2 tbsp) finely chopped parsley
30 ml (2 tbsp) finely chopped chives
30 ml (2 tbsp) finely chopped fennel leaves

Poach or steam the fish until just done. Season and keep warm. Melt butter, add almonds and allow to brown – keep the heat low so that the butter does not burn. Add remaining ingredients, and stir until heated through. Drain any juices that may have escaped from the fish, pour butter sauce over the top, and serve.
Serves 4.

CHILLI FISH PAPRIKA

This recipe confirms the fuss-free pleasure of baking fish in a tasty sauce and is a good choice for entertaining, as the sauce may be made in advance, leaving only the fish needing last-minute attention.

30 ml (2 tbsp) sunflower oil
1 medium onion, chopped
200 g white mushrooms, wiped and thinly sliced
5 ml (1 tsp) paprika
1–2 ml (¼–½ tsp) chilli powder
30 ml (2 tbsp) flour
250 ml (1 cup) hot fish or chicken stock
20 ml (4 tsp) tomato paste
a pinch each of salt and sugar
60 ml (¼ cup) cultured sour cream
4 white fish fillets (about 600 g), skinned
lightly seasoned flour
chopped parsley or garlic chives to garnish

Heat oil, add onion and fry until golden. Add mushrooms and toss until softening, then sprinkle in paprika, chilli powder and flour, keeping the heat low. When absorbed, stir in stock, tomato paste and seasoning, and, when just bubbling and thickened, remove from the stove and stir in cream. Initially it may curdle, but it soon smooths out. If working ahead, set aside at this stage.

Dust fish on both sides with the flour (do this just before baking) and arrange in a well-buttered baking dish to fit closely without overlapping. Spoon sauce over to cover the fish evenly and then bake, uncovered, in the oven at 180 °C for 25–30 minutes or until the sauce is gently bubbling and the fish cooked through – the exact time depends on the thickness of the fillets and whether they are fresh or cooked from frozen. Garnish and serve right away.
Serves 4.

ROSEMARY SAUCE WITH SUN-DRIED TOMATOES FOR BEEF STEAKS

Sauces which are cooked and served separately from the accompanying steaks are always useful because, as the one is not dependent on the other, any preferred cuts of beef can be used, and you can grill or fry them, plate them, and then serve the sauce on the side. Not quite as quick as a pat of herbed butter – but much more seductive.*

1 x 400 g can tomatoes, chopped, plus juice
60 ml (15 g) sun-dried tomatoes, rinsed and slivered
60 ml (¼ cup) red wine
125 ml (½ cup) beef stock
2 ml (½ tsp) salt
7 ml (1½ tsp) sugar
1 small onion, finely chopped
5 ml (1 tsp) chopped fresh rosemary leaves
1 yellow pepper, seeded and diced
30 ml (2 tbsp) soft butter
2 cloves garlic, crushed
15 ml (1 tbsp) flour

Place all the ingredients except the butter, garlic and flour in a saucepan. Bring to the boil, stirring, then reduce heat to very low and simmer, covered, for 15 minutes, stirring once or twice. Mash the butter to a paste with the garlic and flour, and add to the sauce in little pats, stirring until it is blended and the sauce has thickened.
Sufficient for 4 large steaks.

* This is also a super sauce for pasta. Ladle it over servings of tagliatelle or spaghetti, and serve with grated Parmesan cheese.

CRUMBED FILLET STEAKS WITH AVOCADO PURÉE

A recipe for cooks who enjoy pampering guests with this ultimate cut of beef, but who balk at the last-minute frying usually required. This non-gourmet method unashamedly breaks the rules, but it's practical and it's good.

60 ml (¼ cup) mayonnaise
2–3 cloves garlic, crushed
10 ml (2 tsp) wholegrain mustard
5 ml (1 tsp) finely chopped fresh rosemary leaves
6 small beef fillet steaks (about 600 g), 2 cm thick
90 ml (6 tbsp) packaged golden breadcrumbs
2 ml (½ tsp) salt

Mix mayonnaise, garlic, mustard and rosemary, and coat steaks thickly on both sides, then coat with crumbs mixed with salt. Arrange on a large plate and refrigerate for at least 1 hour.
Preheat oven to 220 °C. Place steaks, not touching, in a baking dish lined with baking paper (not waxed or greaseproof paper). Turn the oven down to 200 °C and bake the steaks for about 15 minutes – the time depends on how rare you like them – then switch off the oven and leave for a few minutes to settle. Place on a heated platter and serve immediately.
Serves 4–6.

AVOCADO PURÉE

2 medium, ripe avocados, diced
10 ml (2 tsp) lemon juice
1 small clove garlic, crushed
a pinch of salt
2 spring onions, chopped
60 ml (¼ cup) thick, Bulgarian yoghurt or sour cream

Using a silver fork, mash all the ingredients until smooth, or purée in a blender.

ONE-STEP BEEF CASSEROLE

A strikingly easy recipe devised for flustered cooks. Although the cooking period is lengthy, the preparation could hardly be quicker and, although pre-browning of the meat and onions has been side-stepped, this robust stew has a marvellous flavour with a smack of French cuisine. Serve with couscous.

600 g beef goulash (diced topside or thick flank, lean and boneless)
2 large onions, chopped
3 pickling onions each stuck with 1 whole clove
3 cloves garlic, crushed
2 bay leaves
a handful of chopped parsley
15 ml (1 tbsp) Worcestershire sauce
5 ml (1 tsp) salt and a grind of black pepper
125 ml (½ cup) red wine
125 ml (½ cup) beef stock
30 ml (2 tbsp) brandy
2 large carrots, diced
5 ml (1 tsp) dried thyme
1 slice brown bread, crumbled
30 ml (2 tbsp) tomato paste
5 ml (1 tsp) sugar
250 g button mushrooms, wiped
125 ml (½ cup) red wine, extra triangles of fried bread and chopped parsley to garnish

Mix all ingredients, except mushrooms and extra wine, in a medium-sized baking dish. Cover very securely and bake on the middle shelf of the oven at 160 °C for 1 hour 45 minutes.
Stir in mushrooms and extra wine, cover and bake for a further 45 minutes, by which time the meat should be very tender and the gravy thick and dark brown. If extra thickening is needed, use a touch of cornflour or potato flour – simply stir the latter in over heat, without previous slaking.*
Remove bay leaves and pickling onions, turn into a heated serving dish, arrange fried bread round the sides, and sprinkle with parsley.
Serves 4 generously.

* Wine-based stews are usually even better if reheated. Use a glass or ceramic baking dish, set aside, and, if thickening, do so only when reheating.

BEEF STEAKS WITH RED WINE AND MUSHROOM SAUCE

The chunky, mahogany-coloured sauce is the starring item in this recipe. It is quick, dependable, and just perfect for saucing cooked steaks. Grill or fry the steak of your choice according to taste, and then season and keep warm while the sauce is prepared.

30 ml (2 tbsp) sunflower oil
30 ml (2 tbsp) butter
1 medium onion, finely chopped
30 ml (2 tbsp) flour
125 ml (½ cup) red wine
500 ml (2 cups) beef stock
2–3 cloves garlic, crushed
15 ml (1 tbsp) tomato paste
5 ml (1 tsp) sugar
200 g brown mushrooms, wiped and finely chopped
10 ml (2 tsp) soy sauce

Heat oil and butter in a large frying pan, add onion and brown lightly, then sprinkle in flour. When absorbed, add remaining ingredients except mushrooms and soy sauce, and stir over low heat for a few minutes to thicken and to mellow the wine.
   Add mushrooms and soy sauce, and allow to bubble gently, just until mushrooms have softened, then add any juices that may have collected under the waiting steaks. Pour over and serve.
The sauce is sufficient to transform 4 T-bones, 6 portions of rump or porterhouse, or 8 slices of fillet.

Always wipe meat and poultry with vinegar or vinegar-water before cooking.

SPICY MINCE AND LENTIL CURRY

Home-ground curry powders are always the best, but busy cooks rely on commercial brands. Most of these respond well to the addition of extra spices, and the following is a prime example. Although this can be classed as a budget dish, it is wonderfully fragrant and tasty.

60 ml (¼ cup) sunflower oil
20 ml (4 tsp) butter
2 onions, finely chopped
4 cloves garlic, crushed
20 ml (4 tsp) curry powder
10 ml (2 tsp) each ground coriander, cumin and turmeric
4 star anise
600 g lean beef mince
2 x 400 g cans tomatoes, finely chopped, plus juice
250 ml (180 g) red lentils, rinsed
750 ml (3 cups) beef stock
2 sticks cinnamon
10 ml (2 tsp) each salt and sugar
30 ml (2 tbsp) tomato paste
4 x 250 ml shredded spinach (180 g)
fresh coriander leaves to garnish

In a really large frying pan (failing which, use a wide-based saucepan) heat oil and butter. Add onions, garlic and spices (except cinnamon) and sizzle gently for a few minutes. Reduce heat, add mince, and toss until lightly browned. Add remaining ingredients, slowly bring to the boil while stirring, then cover and simmer on very low heat, stirring occasionally, for 20–25 minutes. The mixture should be thick, but moist – if necessary tilt the lid of the pan for the last few minutes to simmer away excess liquid. Remove cinnamon and anise, turn into a large, heated dish, garnish, and serve.
Serves 8.

PORK CHOPS IN APPLE SAUCE

Slow-baked on a bed of fresh apple slices laced with lemon, sage and a tot of brandy, these chops are then blanketed with the flavoursome apple purée, and the result is light but surprisingly luscious.

8 large rib or loin pork chops
4 large Golden Delicious apples
30 ml (2 tbsp) sunflower oil
salt and pepper
60 ml (¼ cup) water
30 ml (2 tbsp) brandy
5 ml (1 tsp) finely grated lemon rind
30 ml (2 tbsp) finely chopped fresh sage leaves
40 ml (8 tsp) sour cream
ground cinnamon

Remove rind and almost all the fat from the chops. Peel apples, core and slice thinly. Heat oil and lightly brown chops, in relays, on both sides.

Cover base of a large baking dish with apple slices – use a deep dish, to take the layers, as well as a lid that won't rest on the chops. Arrange chops on apples – they should fit closely without overlapping. Season lightly. Mix water and brandy and pour over the chops, then sprinkle with lemon rind and sage. Drizzle 5 ml (1 tsp) sour cream over each chop, and dust with cinnamon.

Cover securely and bake on the middle shelf of the oven at 160 °C for 1 hour 15 minutes, or until chops are cooked through and tender, and the apples have cooked to a juicy mixture.

Transfer chops to a large serving dish. Cool apple sauce briefly, then tip with all the juices into a blender and purée until smooth. Pour this creamy, butterscotch-coloured sauce over the chops and return to the oven until heated through and just beginning to bubble.
Serves 8.

CASSEROLE OF VEAL WITH BRINJALS AND OLIVES

The following recipe is not unlike Italian Osso Buco, but with chunky Mediterranean vegetables adding their individual character and delicious flavour.

1 kg veal shin, sliced into 2 cm slices (10–12 slices)
seasoned flour
olive oil
1 x 400 g can tomatoes, chopped, plus juice
500 g brinjals (2 medium), cubed and dégorged
3 sticks table celery, sliced
12 pickling onions, peeled
15 ml (1 tbsp) tomato paste
7 ml (1½ tsp) dried tarragon
125 ml (½ cup) white wine
250 ml (1 cup) chicken stock
5 ml (1 tsp) salt
10 ml (2 tsp) sugar
6 cloves garlic, peeled
3 bay leaves
black olives (as many as you like)
chopped parsley, fresh tarragon or basil to garnish

Nick edges of shin, roll in seasoned flour, and brown on both sides in a little oil in a frying pan – do this in batches – then arrange in a large baking dish in a single layer.

Add remaining ingredients, except olives, to the pan, stir to mix, then cover and simmer for 10 minutes. Pour over veal, pushing the onions in between the slices, cover securely, and bake at 160 °C for 1½ hours, by which time the veal should be butter-soft, the vegetables cooked, and the sauce rich and thick. Stir in olives and, if necessary, a little extra stock, and return to oven, uncovered, until bubbling. Remove bay leaves and sprinkle with herbs.
Serves 6.

CASSEROLE OF LAMB WITH MUSHROOMS AND BUTTER BEANS

There's a smack of French country village in this earthy stew, brimming with tender nuggets of lamb and vegetables in a thick, herby gravy. Preparation is surprisingly quick, the baking very slow, and interference from the cook virtually nil, yet the result is simply delicious.

1,1 kg lamb knuckles (20–24), sliced 3–4 cm thick*
seasoned flour
sunflower or olive oil
4 cloves garlic
2 large onions, coarsely chopped
3 medium carrots, sliced
5 ml (1 tsp) each dried thyme and origanum
125 ml (½ cup) red wine
200 ml (⅘ cup) beef stock
200 ml (⅘ cup) tomato purée
125 ml (½ cup) parsley tufts
10 ml (2 tsp) Worcestershire sauce
5 ml (1 tsp) salt
10 ml (2 tsp) soft brown sugar
200 g brown mushrooms, wiped and chopped
4 bay leaves
1 x 410 g can butter beans, drained

Roll knuckles in seasoned flour or shake up in a bag – the easiest way. Brown in batches on both sides in a little oil, and then transfer to a large baking dish – 20 x 30 cm is perfect.

Place remaining ingredients, except mushrooms, bay leaves and beans, in a processor fitted with a metal blade and pulse until vegetables are finely chopped. Add mushrooms and then spread over the knuckles.

Tuck in the bay leaves, cover really securely, and bake at 160 °C for 1 hour, then turn and toss knuckles – juices will have drawn, but the meat will not yet be tender, and the flavour of the sauce will not have mellowed. Cover and bake for a further hour, then add beans and bake, uncovered, for about 15 minutes or until sauce has thickened sufficiently. Remove bay leaves. **Serves 6.**

* Do not substitute 'stewing' lamb as it is much too fatty.

MEAT

ITALIAN CASSEROLE OF LAMB

Lamb knuckles become wonderfully tender when slow-baked in a sauce of wine and vegetables. Sprinkled with gremolata and served with risotto, this stew is high on flavour and fairly low in cost.

1 kg lamb knuckles, sliced 2 cm thick, each with a little marrow bone
60 ml (4 tbsp) seasoned flour
60 ml (¼ cup) sunflower oil
15 ml (1 tbsp) butter
2 medium onions, chopped
2 cloves garlic, crushed
2 sticks table celery, chopped
4 medium carrots, diced
500 g juicy tomatoes, skinned and chopped
125 ml (½ cup) white wine
250 ml (1 cup) beef stock
a pinch of sugar
7 ml (1½ tsp) finely chopped fresh rosemary leaves

GREMOLATA
5 ml (1 tsp) finely grated lemon rind
90 ml (6 tbsp) finely chopped parsley
1–2 cloves garlic, crushed

Coat knuckles on both sides with seasoned flour. Heat oil and butter in a large frying pan, add lamb in batches and brown well. Remove to a large baking dish – the knuckles should not fit too closely to allow space for the chunky sauce. Sprinkle any remaining seasoned flour over the knuckles, which must lie flat in the baking dish so that the marrow does not escape.

Add onions, garlic, celery and carrots to the pan with, if necessary, an extra dash of oil or a little water if dry, and toss over low heat for a minute or two, then add remaining ingredients. Bring to the boil, and then pour sauce over lamb.

Cover securely and bake at 160 °C for 1 hour. Carefully turn the knuckles – which should nestle in the bountiful sauce – and bake at 160 °C for a further 30 minutes or until very tender. Check the seasoning, mix the ingredients for the gremolata, sprinkle over the top, and serve. **Serves 5–6.**

When using fresh chillies, it is best to work under a running cold tap. Tug out the stem to remove it, slit one side and, using a sharp-tipped knife, scrape out the fiery seeds, then slice the chilli as required. Juices can burn the eyes and face, so do not touch them while working, and wash your hands afterwards, or wear gloves. The heat of chillies varies a great deal: sometimes the smallest are the hottest, and usually red chillies are hotter than green. In my recipes, I have used the large, fresh, banana-shaped chillies, which are really quite mild as chillies go.

SHERRIED MUSTARD SAUCE

A piquant sauce to drizzle over grilled lamb chops or beef steaks.

30 ml (2 tbsp) soft butter
15 ml (1 tbsp) flour
15 ml (1 tbsp) sunflower oil
2 spring onions, chopped
1 clove garlic, crushed
a small pinch of dried tarragon
200 ml (⁴⁄₅ cup) light beef stock
60 ml (¼ cup) sweet sherry
10 ml (2 tsp) wholegrain mustard

Mash half butter with flour. Heat remaining butter and oil and soften onions, garlic and tarragon. Add stock, sherry and mustard, and simmer, uncovered, for 5 minutes. Add butter-flour paste in small pieces while stirring, and when sauce is smooth and thick, taste, and add a pinch of sugar to round out the flavour. **Makes 200 ml (⁴⁄₅ cup).**

POULTRY

ORANGE COQ AU VIN

A simplified version of this classic dish with a new twist to the flavour.

1 kg chicken portions*
15 ml (1 tbsp) sunflower oil
a dab of butter
salt and pepper
3–4 rashers lean shoulder bacon, diced
12 pickling onions, peeled
2–3 cloves garlic, crushed
30 ml (2 tbsp) flour
2 ml (½ tsp) dried thyme
175 ml (⅔ cup) red wine
125 ml (½ cup) fresh orange juice
5 ml (1 tsp) finely grated orange rind
30 ml (2 tbsp) brandy
15 ml (1 tbsp) tomato paste
60 ml (¼ cup) chicken stock
5 ml (1 tsp) honey
2 bay leaves
200 g button mushrooms, halved
chopped parsley to garnish

Trim chicken pieces of any excess fat. Heat oil and butter and brown chicken on both sides – fry in batches if necessary, and do skin side first. Remove to a baking dish – not too large, or the sauce will boil away, and not too small, or ingredients will not fit. Season. Add bacon, onions and garlic to the pan, toss over low heat, and, when onions are browned, sprinkle in flour and thyme, crushed between the fingers. When absorbed, add remaining ingredients except mushrooms. Stir until boiling, then pour sauce over chicken, tucking in the onions.

Cover, and bake at 160 °C for 1¼ hours. Stir in mushrooms and bake, uncovered, for 15 minutes. If possible, cool down, skim off any fat, and reheat at 160 °C, until bubbling. Remove bay leaves, and garnish with chopped parsley.
Serves 4–5.

*Thighs and drumsticks are best.

FLAMBÉED CHICKEN IN CREAMY GARLIC AND MUSTARD SAUCE

A choice recipe for creamed chicken breasts. The sauce is a blend of finely balanced flavours, and the brandy adds a delicate – yet discernible – spirit to the chicken. Serve prettily plated with rice timbales and bright vegetables.

4 skinless chicken breast fillets (400 g)
2 ml (½ tsp) dried thyme
seasoned flour
15 ml (1 tbsp) sunflower oil
5 ml (1 tsp) butter
30 ml (2 tbsp) brandy, warmed
250 ml (1 cup) chicken stock
2 cloves garlic, crushed
125 ml (½ cup) thick cream
30 ml (2 tbsp) chopped chives
15 ml (1 tbsp) Dijon mustard
5 ml (1 tsp) cornflour

Flatten chicken breasts slightly, rub in thyme, dust with seasoned flour, and brown lightly on both sides in heated oil and butter. Use a medium-sized frying pan that takes the chicken comfortably without crowding. Flame with brandy – be careful here, this quantity of brandy flames quite fiercely. Immediately reduce heat, add the stock and garlic, cover, and simmer the chicken gently for about 8 minutes or until cooked through. Using a slotted spoon, remove chicken to a serving dish and keep warm. Stir together cream, half the chives, mustard and cornflour, add to juices in the pan, and bring to the boil, stirring. Allow to bubble gently for a few minutes, until slightly reduced and thickened, then pour over the chicken, and sprinkle with remaining chives.
Serves 4.

WALNUT CHICKEN SALAD WITH CORIANDER YOGHURT

Shades of Turkish and Asian cuisine blend harmoniously in this gently spiced salad. The combination is light, bright, low-fat and refreshing, and makes a splendid summer lunch. Add your favourite rice salad, or bulgur or couscous for ethnic appeal.

500 g skinless chicken breast fillets
5 ml (1 tsp) each ground cumin, coriander and turmeric
2 ml (½ tsp) salt
500 ml (2 cups) stirred Bulgarian yoghurt
60 ml (¼ cup) cultured sour cream
15 ml (1 tbsp) honey
30 ml (2 tbsp) chopped fresh coriander leaves*
salt and pepper
lightly toasted walnuts, coarsely chopped

Place chicken in a single layer in a shallow, wide-based frying pan – the fillets should just cover the base. Sprinkle with spices and salt, then add just enough water to cover – about 150 ml (⅔ cup). Bring to the boil, then cover and simmer for 8–10 minutes, until chicken is cooked, turning once. Leave to cool in the stock, then slice into thin strips across the grain, and place in a shallow serving dish. Return pan to the stove and boil the spicy stock on high heat until reduced to about 30 ml (2 tbsp). Add to yoghurt, then stir in sour cream, honey, coriander and a pinch of seasoning. Pour over chicken, tossing gently to combine. Stand for about 15 minutes, or refrigerate. Just before serving sprinkle generously with walnuts. **Serves 6.**

* If refrigerating the dish for more than an hour or two, use slightly less coriander as the flavour will gradually become more dominant.

TROPICAL CHICKEN IN CURRY CREAM

An unusually delicate curry with an exotic flavour.

6 skinless chicken breast fillets
60 ml (4 tbsp) desiccated coconut with a little salt
1 large, fibreless mango, sliced into thin strips
30 ml (2 tbsp) sunflower oil
1 onion, finely chopped
5 ml (1 tsp) chopped, peeled root ginger
2 ml (½ tsp) each turmeric and ground cumin
15 ml (1 tbsp) curry powder
30 ml (2 tbsp) flour
375 ml (1½ cups) chicken stock
125 ml (½ cup) thick cream
2 ml (½ tsp) finely grated lemon rind
5 ml (1 tsp) honey
garam masala to garnish

Roll chicken breasts in coconut as you would with seasoned flour. Arrange in a lightly oiled baking dish, allowing just enough room between breasts to slip in the mango.

To make the sauce, heat the oil, add onion and spices, and toss until onion has softened and spices smell good. Keep heat low so as not to scorch – you might have to add a dash of water. Sprinkle in flour and, when absorbed, add stock and bring to a slow boil, stirring.

When thickened, add cream, lemon rind and honey. Check for salt – the amount depends on the saltiness of the stock – and then pour sauce over chicken and mango. The sauce should cover them completely.

Bake, uncovered, in the oven at 160 °C for about 40 minutes, or until the sauce is bubbling and the chicken is cooked through. Sprinkle with the garam masala.

Serves 4–5.

SPICY CHICKEN CURRY SUPREME

As the title implies, this is a favourite curried chicken casserole. Abundantly perfumed and flavoured, its finest mate is delicate Basmati rice. Accompany the curry with an array of tasty sambals, or simply add a couple of star anise, whole cloves and a stick of cinnamon when boiling long-grain white rice.

45 ml (3 tbsp) flour
7 ml (1½ tsp) salt
5 ml (1 tsp) garam masala
8 skinless chicken thighs (about 1 kg)
30 ml (2 tbsp) sunflower oil
2 medium onions, chopped
2–3 cloves garlic, crushed
10 ml (2 tsp) chopped, peeled root ginger, or 5 ml (1 tsp) ground ginger
15 ml (1 tbsp) curry powder
5 ml (1 tsp) each ground cumin and turmeric
3 star anise
2 sticks cinnamon
300 ml (1⅕ cups) chicken stock
125 ml (½ cup) tomato purée
2 bay leaves
60 ml (4 tbsp) seedless raisins
30 ml (2 tbsp) chutney

Mix flour, salt and garam masala, and rub into the chicken thighs. Arrange in a lightly oiled baking dish to fit quite snugly, and sprinkle any remaining seasoned flour mixture over the chicken thighs.

Heat the oil, add onions and garlic, and fry lightly. Add all the spices and stir over low heat until the aroma escapes – if necessary, add a dash of water to prevent scorching. Add the remaining ingredients, stir while heating through, then pour over the chicken.

Check that the spices lie in the sauce and not on top of the chicken, then cover and bake at 160 °C for 45 minutes.

Turn the chicken and bake, covered, for a further 30 minutes or until tender. Transfer to a heated serving dish, as the baking dish will be spattered, or, if time allows, allow to cool for the full flavour to develop, then remove spices and bay leaves and reheat, covered, at 160 °C for about 30 minutes, until bubbling. If necessary, add extra chicken stock before reheating to make sure that the chicken curry is saucy enough to serve with rice.
Serves 4–6.

CHICKEN MYKONOS

Greek cuisine is characterised by distinctive flavours, and this lemony, spicy and herby chicken is a spirited example. Choose one of the side dishes to complement the zesty chicken.

800 g chicken thighs, trimmed of excess fat
a little salt
60 ml (¼ cup) lemon juice
30 ml (2 tbsp) olive oil
15 ml (1 tbsp) brandy
15 ml (1 tbsp) honey
2 cloves garlic, crushed
7 ml (1½ tsp) ground cumin
7 ml (1½ tsp) dried origanum
2 ml (½ tsp) ground cinnamon

Arrange chicken in a baking dish to fit closely. Mix ingredients for marinade, pour over chicken and refrigerate for 4 hours, turning a few times. Unless using a fridge-to-oven dish, return to room temperature before baking.
Arrange chicken pieces skin side up, salt lightly, and bake, uncovered, at 160 °C for 45 minutes. Baste with the juices in the dish, then continue baking for a further 25 minutes or until browned and tender. Transfer chicken to a heated platter and spoon the juices over.
Serves 4.

HONEYED PEPPERS AND BRINJAL
Prepare while the chicken is baking.

1 small brinjal (150 g) washed and cubed, not peeled
1 each large red and yellow pepper, seeded and julienned
1 medium onion, sliced into thin rings
2–3 cloves garlic, crushed
30 ml (2 tbsp) lemon juice
30 ml (2 tbsp) olive oil
15 ml (1 tbsp) honey
60 ml (¼ cup) water
2 ml (½ tsp) each salt, ground cumin and coriander
crumbled feta cheese or Bulgarian yoghurt for topping

Place all ingredients in a wide-based frying pan, bring to the boil, then cover and simmer gently, stirring occasionally, until vegetables are cooked but still juicy. Top with cheese or yoghurt.
Serves 4.

GLAZED BABY ONIONS
500 g pickling onions
250 ml (1 cup) chicken stock
15 ml (1 tbsp) butter
30 ml (2 tbsp) currants
2 ml (½ tsp) salt
15 ml (1 tbsp) honey
2 bay leaves
15 ml (1 tbsp) tomato paste
a few sprigs of fresh thyme

Place onions in a wide-based saucepan, cover with cold water, bring to the boil, then simmer briefly, cool and slip off skins. Bring remaining ingredients to the boil, add onions, reduce heat, then cover and simmer until tender. Remove bay leaves and thyme.
Serves 4.

Do not cool or store curries or stews in metallic containers.

CHUTNEY CHICKEN WITH ORANGE

They don't come simpler than this, and yet the flavour is excellent. Team with yellow rice and broccoli for a beautifully bright presentation. When baking chicken pieces without browning them first, it is important to trim off all fat, or it will cook into the sauce; they will also take longer to cook than pre-fried chicken.

1 kg chicken thighs, trimmed

SAUCE
125 ml (½ cup) mild fruit chutney
250 ml (1 cup) fresh orange juice
60 ml (¼ cup) water
5 ml (1 tsp) finely grated orange rind
2 ml (½ tsp) each ground cinnamon and ginger
5 ml (1 tsp) salt
30 ml (2 tbsp) flour

Arrange thighs, skin side up, in a single layer in a baking dish brushed with oil – the dish should be just large enough to accommodate thighs and sauce without crowding. Remember that ovenproof glass is preferable when making a sweetish sauce, as it is less likely to scorch. Mix ingredients for sauce, stirring well to incorporate the flour. Pour over chicken. Cover, and bake at 160 °C for 1 hour. Baste well, and add a little extra water if necessary. Return to oven and bake, uncovered, for another 15–20 minutes, until browned and tender.
Serves 4–5.

CHICKEN STIR-FRY WITH LITCHIS AND GINGER

Like most stir-fries, this is not easy to do for a crowd because the ingredients are bulky and even though you can assemble them in advance, they must be cooked at the last minute. However, this one's so good that it's worth tossing up for some special diners.

1 x 410 g can pitted litchis in syrup
45 ml (3 tbsp) sunflower oil
400 g skinless chicken breast fillets, sliced across the grain
3 leeks, thinly sliced
2 cloves garlic, crushed
10 ml (2 tsp) finely chopped, peeled root ginger
5 ml (1 tsp) ground coriander
1 red pepper, seeded and diced
125 g mangetout, topped and tailed
2 sticks table celery, plus some leaves, chopped
½ English cucumber (about 300 g), pared, seeded and julienned
30 ml (2 tbsp) soy sauce
60 ml (¼ cup) medium-dry sherry
10 ml (2 tsp) lemon juice
125 ml (½ cup) reserved litchi syrup
125 ml (½ cup) chicken stock
15 ml (1 tbsp) cornflour
roasted cashew nuts to garnish

Drain the litchis and slice. Heat the oil in a large wok or frying pan, add the chicken, leeks, garlic, ginger and coriander, and stir-fry until the chicken is just cooked. The heat should be kept low to prevent drying out. Add all the vegetables and toss for about 5 minutes, until crisp-tender. Mix the remaining ingredients, except the litchis, add to the pan, and allow to boil up and thicken. Stir in the litchis and heat through. Top with the nuts and serve on rice.
Serves 4.

LOW-KILOJOULE CHICKEN WITH CHUNKY VEGETABLES

A light dish of chicken poached on a bed of vegetables – this is a super recipe and excellent proof that tasty food need be neither fussy nor fattening. Serve with rice or thin noodles and a salad of spinach and sprouts.

5 ml (1 tsp) honey
5 ml (1 tsp) ground ginger
1 ml (¼ tsp) salt
15 ml (1 tbsp) prepared mustard
4 skinless chicken breast fillets (350–400 g)
250 ml (1 cup) chicken stock
2 cloves garlic, crushed
2 large brown mushrooms (about 90 g), wiped and sliced
4 baby marrows (about 125 g), pared and diced
15 ml (1 tbsp) soy sauce
5 ml (1 tsp) ground coriander
2 leeks, thinly sliced
15 ml (1 tbsp) sunflower oil
10 ml (2 tsp) cornflour slaked with 15 ml (1 tbsp) water
toasted sesame seeds to garnish

Mix honey, ginger, salt and mustard, use to coat both sides of the chicken breasts, and leave to stand for 1 hour.

Place remaining ingredients, except cornflour and water, in a large, wide-based frying pan, stir to mix, bring to the boil, and place the chicken on top. Reduce heat immediately, then cover and simmer gently for about 15 minutes or until the chicken is just cooked and the vegetables have softened.

Remove the chicken to a heated platter and thicken the sauce with the slaked cornflour. Pour the sauce over the chicken, and sprinkle with sesame seeds. **Serves 4.**

ALMOND CHICKEN IN A CREAMY MUSTARD AND WHISKY SAUCE

If the budget is tight, omit the almonds – the chicken will still have an engaging flavour.

4 filleted, skinless chicken breasts (450 g)
45 ml (3 tbsp) ground almonds
2 ml (½ tsp) salt
15 ml (1 tbsp) sunflower oil
a nut of butter
10 ml (2 tsp) yellow mustard seeds
30 ml (2 tbsp) flour
200 ml (⁴⁄₅ cup) hot chicken stock
15 ml (1 tbsp) wholegrain mustard
125 ml (½ cup) sour cream
10 ml (2 tsp) honey
30 ml (2 tbsp) whisky
toasted slivered almonds to garnish

Flatten chicken breasts slightly and dust on both sides with ground almonds mixed with salt.

Heat oil and butter, add chicken and fry quickly on both sides, just to seal without browning. Remove from the pan and set aside.

Keeping heat very low, sprinkle mustard seeds into pan – if all juices have been absorbed, add a dash of oil.

As soon as seeds begin to sizzle and pop – this happens very quickly – stir in flour, then slowly stir in stock and, when thickening, add mustard, cream and honey. When the sauce is smooth, return the chicken and add whisky.

Cover and simmer very gently for about 10 minutes or until the chicken is just cooked through, turning once.

Arrange the chicken in a heated serving dish, pour the sauce over, and top with the slivered almonds. **Makes 4 modest portions.**

EASTERN CHICKEN WITH MUSHROOMS AND CORIANDER

This dish was inspired by a superb Korma I enjoyed at an Indian restaurant in, surprisingly, a foggy little village in Yorkshire. It is a bright and fragrant dish, for which you must have fresh coriander.

5 ml (1 tsp) each ground ginger, cumin, garam masala and turmeric
1 ml (¼ tsp) chilli powder
5 ml (1 tsp) salt
500 g skinless chicken breast fillets
30 ml (2 tbsp) sunflower oil
1 large onion, finely chopped
2 cloves garlic, crushed
375 ml (1½ cups) chicken stock
200 g white mushrooms, wiped and sliced
45 ml (3 tbsp) sultanas
45 ml (3 tbsp) chopped fresh coriander leaves
15 ml (1 tbsp) cornflour
75 ml (5 tbsp) cream
a little lemon juice
roasted cashew nuts to garnish

Mix spices and dry-roast for a minute or two on medium heat in a non-stick frying pan, then mix with salt and rub well into both sides of chicken. Set aside for 1 hour, or refrigerate for longer. Just before cooking, slice chicken fillets into thin strips across the grain. Heat oil in a large frying pan, add onion and garlic, toss until softening, then stir in chicken. Add stock and mushrooms, cover, and simmer gently for 10–15 minutes, until chicken is cooked. Add sultanas, coriander and cornflour slaked with the cream. Simmer, uncovered, until very hot and sauce has thickened sufficiently. Check seasoning, add a dash of lemon juice to sharpen the flavour, turn into a heated serving dish, and sprinkle with cashews. Serves 4.

CHICKEN MARSALA

Although the ingredients are reasonably basic, the flavours in this chicken dish come together beautifully. This dish is easy to prepare, and certainly good enough for last-minute company. Serve with buttered rice or pasta, and a green salad.

6 skinless chicken breast fillets (about 600 g)
30 ml (2 tbsp) sunflower oil
15 ml (1 tbsp) butter
1 medium onion, finely chopped
5 ml (1 tsp) dried tarragon
75 ml (5 tbsp) sweet sherry
375 ml (1½ cups) chicken stock
15 ml (1 tbsp) tomato paste
200 g white mushrooms, wiped and sliced
2 ml (½ tsp) salt
30 ml (2 tbsp) cornflour
75 ml (5 tbsp) cultured sour cream
fresh tarragon or snipped chives to garnish

Flatten the chicken breasts slightly with the heel of your hand. Heat oil and butter in a large frying pan and quickly seal breasts on both sides – do not brown. Remove and set aside.

Reduce the heat, add onion and tarragon to the pan, and, when softening, add sherry. Bubble for 1 minute, then add the stock, tomato paste, mushrooms and salt. Bring to the boil, stirring, then return the chicken to the pan, spooning the sauce over the top.

Cover and simmer very gently for about 10 minutes, until just cooked through. Slake cornflour with cream, add to pan and allow to thicken, uncovered. Check seasoning, spoon into a heated serving dish, and garnish with tarragon or chives. Serves 4–6.

POULTRY 41

CHICKEN IN APPLE AND MUSTARD CREAM SAUCE

Bestow your personal preferences on this dish and make it entirely your own. Golden Delicious apples will cloak the chicken in a sweetish sauce; Granny Smith apples will add their individual tang.

800 g skinned chicken thighs
seasoned flour
30 ml (2 tbsp) Dijon mustard
2 apples (total weight 250 g), peeled and slivered
250 ml (1 cup) unsweetened apple juice
a large pinch of ground cinnamon
100 ml (²/₅ cup) thick cream
about 15 ml (1 tbsp) cornflour
30 ml (2 tbsp) brandy (optional)

Roll thighs in seasoned flour until completely coated. Arrange, rounded sides up, in a buttered baking dish to fit without overlapping – a deep, 23 cm pie dish is just right. Spread mustard over chicken. Add apple slices, pressing them right down between the thighs. Pour apple juice over. Dust with cinnamon. Bake, covered, at 180 °C for 1 hour 10 minutes, until tender. Using a slotted spoon, remove chicken to a serving dish with sides to hold the sauce. Cover – as the chicken should not brown – and return to low oven to keep warm. Add cream to juices and purée in a blender until smooth. Rinse a saucepan with water (to prevent scorching), add sauce and either boil, stirring, until reduced, thickened and a rich colour, or thicken with cornflour slaked with brandy, or a little milk if preferred. When sauce is the consistency of thick cream, pour over chicken. Serve 2 thighs per person, generously napped with the sauce.
Serves 4.

PINEAPPLE-SESAME CHICKEN SALAD

Oriental flavours sparkle in this light chicken salad, dressed with a fragrant sesame and ginger dressing instead of mayonnaise. Serve mounded in the centre of a large platter and surround with its perfect companion – Rice Salad with Mushrooms and Sprouts (see page 60).

800 g skinless chicken breast fillets
1 bunch spring onions, chopped
½ English cucumber, pared, seeded and diced
1 large red pepper, seeded and chopped
1 x 440 g can pineapple rings, drained, diced and juice reserved

DRESSING
45 ml (3 tbsp) toasted sesame seeds
200 ml (⁴/₅ cup) sunflower oil
60 ml (¼ cup) lemon juice
2 walnut-sized knobs of root ginger, peeled and chopped
10 ml (2 tsp) dark sesame oil
20 ml (4 tsp) soy sauce
sliced avocado and toasted sesame seeds to garnish

Poach the chicken in lightly salted water with a chopped onion, parsley and 2 bay leaves until just cooked, keeping the liquid at a very gentle simmer. Cool in the stock, then drain and slice thinly across the grain. Mix the chicken with the remaining salad ingredients, toss with 125 ml (½ cup) reserved pineapple juice, and set aside. Place all the ingredients for the dressing in a blender and blend well. Toss with the chicken mixture, cover and refrigerate for an hour or two – it should not be served icy cold. Garnish with avocado slices and sesame seeds just before serving.
Serves 6–8.

PASTA PUTTANESCA SALAD

Rather daring and different, but not at all daunting to the cook. Zesty Puttanesca is usually served hot, but if you increase the quantity of tomatoes to sauce the pasta sufficiently, it makes a bright and lively salad. Serve with a French loaf, sliced to the base but not quite through, lavished with herbed butter, wrapped and baked.

60 ml (¼ cup) olive oil
1 x 50 g can anchovy fillets, drained and briefly soaked in milk*
3 cloves garlic, crushed
4 spring onions, chopped
2 x 400 g cans tomatoes, finely chopped, plus juice
8 each black and green olives, pitted and slivered
1 each fresh red and green chilli, seeded and chopped
1 large yellow pepper, seeded and chopped
125 ml (½ cup) chopped parsley
a little salt
10 ml (2 tsp) sugar
250 g fusilli screws
fresh basil to garnish

Heat olive oil together with the oil from the drained anchovies in a wide frying pan. Add garlic and cook for a few seconds until starting to colour. Add the remaining ingredients except pasta, and simmer on low heat, uncovered and stirring, occasionally, for 10 minutes until it has thickened.

Meanwhile, cook pasta, drain well and turn into a large serving dish. Add sauce and toss until combined. Stand uncovered to cool – the sauce will gradually be absorbed – then cover and leave for up to 2 hours, or refrigerate. Garnish with plenty of basil.
Serves 6.

* Preferably genuine anchovies, not anchovied sardines.

GARDEN VEGETABLE AND HERB FETTUCINE

A fashionably light, fresh and fragrant tangle of pasta, vegetables and fresh herbs.

30 ml (2 tbsp) olive oil
3–4 rashers lean shoulder bacon, diced
1 large onion, chopped
2 cloves garlic, crushed
250 g baby marrows, pared and julienned
1 each red and green pepper, seeded and julienned
2 sticks table celery, plus leaves, chopped
300 g tomatoes, diced but not skinned
250 ml (45 g) shredded spinach
125 ml (½ cup) chopped parsley
5 ml (1 tsp) salt
250 g fettucine
60 ml (4 tbsp) chopped, mixed fresh herbs*
45 ml (3 tbsp) butter
45 ml (3 tbsp) grated Parmesan cheese

Heat oil and fry bacon, onion and garlic until onion softens and bacon starts shrivelling. Add marrows, peppers, celery and a little water, toss over low heat until nearly tender, add tomatoes, spinach, parsley and salt and a little more water if necessary, then cover and cook for about 5 minutes, until the vegetables are just cooked and juicy.

Meanwhile, cook fettucine, and drain well but do not rinse. Tip into a large, heated serving dish, add herbs, butter and cheese, and toss using two forks. Add vegetables and toss again, then serve immediately. Pass extra Parmesan cheese at the table, and a pepper mill.
Serves 4–6.

* Use whatever you have – basil, chives, thyme, sage, marjoram and origanum – but not rosemary.

FETTUCINE WITH MUSHROOMS AND SUN-DRIED TOMATOES

Pasta sauced with tomatoes is nothing new, but when the tomatoes are sun-dried, the dish takes on a different complexion. These shrivelled little red nuggets with their sweet-tart flavour have become hot fashion, and here they are creamily combined with mushrooms.

60 ml (¼ cup) each olive and sunflower oil
2 medium onions, chopped
3–4 leeks, sliced
4 cloves garlic, crushed
500 g brown mushrooms, wiped and chopped
2 yellow peppers, seeded and diced
60 g (about 250 ml) sun-dried tomatoes, rinsed and slivered
2 sprigs rosemary
30 ml (2 tbsp) tomato paste
125 ml (½ cup) red wine
500 ml (2 cups) beef stock
5 ml (1 tsp) salt
10 ml (2 tsp) sugar
400 g fettucine (or spaghetti)
125 ml (½ cup) cultured sour cream

Heat oils in a very large frying pan. Add onions, leeks and garlic and, when golden brown, add mushrooms, peppers, tomatoes and rosemary. Toss until glistening and aromatic, then add remaining ingredients except fettucine and cream. Cover, and simmer on very low heat for 15 minutes, until tomatoes have softened and most of the liquid has been absorbed.

Meanwhile, cook and drain pasta. Remove rosemary from sauce, stir in cream, and simmer, uncovered, for a few minutes to bind and thicken. Serve ladled over servings of cooked pasta, and serve with grated Parmesan.
Serves 6.

PASTA WITH SMOKED SALMON, MUSHROOMS AND CREAM

A dish of pasta, smoked salmon and cream is often featured on the menus of restaurants, and it is dreamy, but so extravagant and rich that one would not usually consider making it at home. This recipe, however, was devised with an eye to scaling the whole lot down, making it possible to serve this delectable combination when the need for indulgence strikes.

500 g white mushrooms, wiped and thinly sliced
6–8 spring onions, chopped
250 ml (1 cup) cream*
250 ml (1 cup) milk
125 ml (½ cup) off-dry white wine
30 ml (2 tbsp) tomato paste
5 ml (1 tsp) salt
30 ml (2 tbsp) cornflour
about 320 g smoked salmon*, sliced into thin strips
400 g fusilli screws*

Put mushrooms and onions in a large saucepan. Stir together the cream, milk, wine, tomato paste, salt and cornflour until smooth, and mix with mushrooms.

Simmer, covered, over low heat for about 10 minutes, until thick and creamy. Stir in salmon and heat through.

Cook the pasta while the sauce is simmering. Drain and place in a large, heated serving dish.

Pour the sauce over the top, toss until combined, and serve immediately with a dressed salad. A pepper mill, passed at the table, is essential.
Serves 6.

* Use the quantities of cream, smoked salmon and pasta as a guide – any or all of them may be increased for larger portions.

HERBED PASTA WITH STIR-FRIED VEGETABLES

A version of Pasta Primavera, this is a joyfully light, colourful and simple mixture of pasta and vegetables, rather like a hot salad. You will need a wok or very large frying pan to accommodate the vegetables, which may be altered according to whatever is in season, using the following merely as a guide to quantity. If vegetables are prepared in advance, the final cook-up will take little time.

60 ml (¼ cup) olive oil
2 medium onions, sliced into thin rings
2 cloves garlic, crushed
250 g baby marrows, pared and sliced
4 medium carrots, julienned
3 sticks table celery, plus some leaves, chopped
1 large red pepper, seeded and julienned
200 g brown mushrooms, wiped and sliced
250 g tomatoes, chopped
125 g mangetout, trimmed
10 ml (2 tsp) salt
a pinch of sugar
125 ml (½ cup) dry white vermouth
250 g elbow macaroni or fusilli
125 ml (½ cup) chopped fresh herbs, including plenty of parsley
black olives, slivered (optional)
diced butter or French dressing
grated Parmesan or crumbled feta cheese

Heat oil (if using a non-stick wok, follow the manufacturer's instructions) and add onions, garlic, marrows, carrots, celery and red pepper. Toss until softening, then add mushrooms, tomatoes, mangetout, seasoning and vermouth. Cover, and simmer briefly on very low heat until vegetables are tender yet retain plenty of character.

Meanwhile, cook pasta, drain, and turn into a large, heated serving dish. Mix in herbs, olives (if using) and either butter or a little lemony French dressing to make it succulent and glossy.

Pour vegetable mixture over the pasta and toss to mix, using two forks. Serve at once with the cheese, freshly ground pepper and hot rolls or pita breads. **Serves 5–6.**

PANZEROTTI WITH MUSHROOM AND WHITE WINE SAUCE

Little pasta dumplings stuffed with spinach and Ricotta, a simple mushroom sauce, and a whiff of nutmeg – the marriage of flavours here is outstanding. Servings should be lavished with Parmesan cheese, and accompanied with Italian bread and a green salad.

30 ml (2 tbsp) sunflower oil
15 ml (1 tbsp) butter
1 medium onion, sliced into thin rings
2 cloves garlic, crushed
300 g white mushrooms, wiped and chopped
45 ml (3 tbsp) flour
375 ml (1½ cups) chicken stock
125 ml (½ cup) semi-sweet white wine
15 ml (1 tbsp) soy sauce
15 ml (1 tbsp) tomato paste
60 ml (4 tbsp) chopped parsley
a pinch each of grated nutmeg, salt and pepper
500 g spinach-and-Ricotta stuffed panzerotti*
grated Parmesan cheese to serve

Heat oil and butter, add onion, garlic and mushrooms, cover and sweat on very low heat for about 10 minutes, until softened. Sprinkle in the flour and, when absorbed, add the remaining ingredients except panzerotti – be a miser with the nutmeg as it can easily be overdone. Cover and simmer for about 10 minutes, stirring occasionally.

Meanwhile, cook panzerotti, drain well, toss with a dash of olive oil, then fold into the sauce and serve immediately with grated Parmesan cheese.
Serves 4.

* If frozen, thaw before cooking or they will probably explode.

ONE-STEP PASTA SAUCES

Two easy but novel recipes for those in search of something a bit different.

NUTTY RICOTTA, TOMATO AND PESTO SAUCE

sun-dried tomatoes in oil
180 g Ricotta cheese
60 ml (4 tbsp) pesto
a handful of chopped walnuts
about 400 g pasta of choice

Drain tomatoes and snip enough to provide 90 ml (6 tbsp) thin slivers. Mix with cheese, pesto and nuts. Cook pasta. Drain, and stir enough of the cooking water into cheese mixture to provide a soft and creamy texture. Add salt to taste. Spoon onto servings of steaming pasta and pass a pepper mill.
Sauce sufficient for about 400 g pasta.

MUSHROOM, BASIL AND CREAM SAUCE

250 g brown mushrooms, wiped and chopped
2 cloves garlic, crushed
1 leek, chopped
60 ml (¼ cup) sweet sherry
125 ml (½ cup) cream
125 ml (½ cup) cultured sour cream
2 ml (½ tsp) salt
15 ml (1 tbsp) cornflour
125 ml (½ cup) chopped basil leaves
chopped walnuts (optional)

Place all the ingredients except half the basil and walnuts, if using, in the top of a double boiler and cook, covered, over simmering water for 30 minutes, stirring occasionally.

Add the remaining chopped basil and walnuts, toss with 300 g cooked, drained pasta of your choice, and serve with grated Parmesan cheese and milled black pepper.
Serves 4.

PESTO

Pesto alla Genovese is possibly the most acclaimed accompaniment to pasta, and it's worth setting aside a corner of your herb garden to grow your own basil.

I make quantities of pesto in summer – it freezes beautifully and means I can serve an instant pasta meal throughout the year. Served on baked potatoes, it also makes a super alternative to sour cream, while a teaspoon or two stirred into minestrone or fish soup adds a special zip to the flavour.

Here are three recipes including – Mamma Mia – a pesto WITHOUT basil. In all the recipes the quantity of olive oil may be reduced to make a thicker, less oily pesto, which can be thinned downed before serving with a little of the water in which the pasta was cooked. This also diminishes the intense flavour for those who prefer a subtler taste.

PERFECT PESTO DE LUXE
Splash out on pine nuts, extra virgin olive oil and freshly grated Parmesan cheese and whizz up this de luxe version.

750 ml (60 g) fresh basil leaves
250 ml (15 g) parsley tufts
1–2 cloves garlic
30 g pine nuts
60 ml (4 tbsp) grated Parmesan cheese
about 125 ml (½ cup) olive oil
a pinch of salt

Rinse and spin-dry basil and parsley, then place in a processor fitted with the metal blade together with garlic, nuts and cheese. Process until very finely chopped, using a rubber spatula to scrape down the sides when necessary. Slowly dribble in the oil while processing, until the mixture becomes a thick, green purée, adding a little salt at the end. Spoon into a glass jar, cover the top with a thin film of oil to preserve the colour, close, and refrigerate. Serve a dollop on each portion of freshly cooked, well-drained pasta, on heated plates.
Makes about 250 ml (1 cup).

ECONOMICAL PESTO
This one is made without expensive pine nuts.

500 ml (40 g) fresh basil leaves
250 ml (15 g) parsley tufts
125 ml (40 g) freshly grated Parmesan cheese
1–2 cloves garlic, chopped
about 125 ml (½ cup) olive oil
a little salt

Place basil, parsley, cheese and garlic in a processor fitted with the metal blade and chop finely. Slowly, while processing, add oil, using just enough to make a thick, creamy mixture. Season and spoon into a glass jar, run a thin film of oil over the top, close and refrigerate.
Makes about 200 ml (⅘ cup).

PESTO FOR ALL SEASONS
This alternative uses perennial herbs.

500 ml (30 g) parsley tufts
75 ml (5 tbsp) fresh herb leaves, e.g. thyme, marjoram, chives, origanum*
1 clove garlic
30 g pine nuts (optional)
60 ml (4 tbsp) freshly grated Parmesan cheese
about 125 ml (½ cup) olive oil
a pinch of salt

To make, follow instructions for Perfect Pesto De Luxe.

* Measure herbs before chopping and washing; use more marjoram and thyme than origanum, and no rosemary.

Stir a little pesto into the French dressing or mayonnaise when making a chicken, tomato or pasta salad – and taste the difference!

HERBED VEGETABLE AND PASTA SALAD

A boisterous salad with an abundance of flavours and variations. Serve simply, with bowls of olives and cubed feta, puffy pitas and basil-dressed tomatoes; or toss in two cans of shredded tuna; or partner the pasta with thick slices of garlicky roast lamb for a Mediterranean-style patio party.

300 g brinjals, cubed and dégorged
300 g young green beans, trimmed and halved
300 g baby marrows, pared and cut into 1 cm rounds
2 red peppers, seeded and diced
300 g brown mushrooms, wiped and cut into chunks
1 large onion, chunkily chopped
60 ml (¼ cup) each sunflower and olive oil
3 cloves garlic, crushed
5 ml (1 tsp) each salt, dried basil and origanum
125 ml (½ cup) water
250 g tri-coloured fusilli
a little French dressing
fresh basil to garnish

Place prepared vegetables in a large glass or porcelain baking dish, about 23 x 28 cm and at least 7 cm deep. Mix the oils, garlic, salt and herbs, pour over vegetables, toss until well mixed, then cover loosely and stand for 1–2 hours. Toss occasionally (and inhale deeply – the aroma at this stage is a knock-out).

To bake, add water and bake in the oven, uncovered, at 200 °C for 35 minutes or until beans and brinjals are tender. Remove from the oven twice during this period and mix lightly to moisten all the vegetables with the juices which have formed. If it is not sufficiently juicy, add a little more water, but be careful not to end up with a stew.

Meanwhile, cook pasta, drain well, and add while hot to the cooked vegetables. Toss gently until everything is beautifully shiny, then cover loosely and cool. Just before serving, toss with French dressing to loosen and gloss the salad, and add a pinch of sugar and/or salt if necessary. Spoon onto a large platter and garnish with basil.
Serves 8.

ORIENTAL SOYA BEANS

Soya beans are extremely nourishing and economical and play a vital part in a vegetarian diet, being a highly concentrated source of protein. But they are bland in flavour and do need help – either tucked into a salad, made into patties, or mixed with vegetables in a tasty sauce as follows.

45 ml (3 tbsp) sunflower oil
1 large onion, chopped
2 cloves garlic, crushed
1 green pepper, seeded and diced
10 ml (2 tsp) chopped, peeled root ginger
200 g brown mushrooms, wiped and sliced
2 sticks table celery, sliced
500 ml (360 g) cooked soya beans
4 rings canned pineapple, drained and diced
200 ml (⁴⁄₅ cup) water
200 ml (⁴⁄₅ cup) pineapple juice (from the can)
30 ml (2 tbsp) soy sauce
5 ml (1 tsp) lemon juice
15 ml (1 tbsp) cornflour
30 ml (2 tbsp) sherry
extra soy sauce and/or lemon juice if necessary
toasted sesame seeds, almonds or cashew nuts to garnish

Heat oil in a large frying pan. Add onion, garlic, green pepper, ginger, mushrooms and celery, and stir-fry until softening. Mix in beans, pineapple, water, juice, soy sauce and lemon juice. Cover and simmer on low heat for 15–20 minutes.

Slake cornflour with sherry, stir into pan and allow to boil up and thicken. Check seasoning, adding a little extra soy sauce or lemon juice if necessary. Turn into a heated serving dish, sprinkle with seeds or nuts, and serve on brown rice tossed with bean sprouts and a knob of butter.
Serves 4–6.

LEBANESE LENTILS

If you like lentils, you'll love this dish, and if you've never liked lentils, this spicy stew might just change your mind. Served on rice, it makes one of the cheapest vegetarian meals possible; add a bowl of mint- or coriander-flavoured yoghurt, and the One-Step Ratatouille (see page 62), and it will also be one of the most delicious.

45 ml (3 tbsp) sunflower oil
1 medium onion, finely chopped
3 cloves garlic, crushed
10 ml (2 tsp) each ground cumin and coriander
375 ml (300 g) brown lentils, picked over and rinsed
2 medium carrots, coarsely grated
2 sticks cinnamon
200 ml (⁴⁄₅ cup) tomato purée
1 litre (4 cups) vegetable stock or water
75 ml (5 tbsp) chopped parsley
75 ml (5 tbsp) currants
5 ml (1 tsp) salt
2 ml (½ tsp) sugar
4 bay leaves

Heat the oil in a large saucepan. Add the onion, garlic and spices, and toss on low heat for a few minutes.

Add the remaining ingredients, bring to the boil, then reduce heat and simmer, covered, for about 50 minutes, stirring the mixture occasionally.

As the lentils swell and soften you will probably need to add up to 250 ml (1 cup) extra stock or water to keep the mixture moist and succulent.

When the lentils are soft, the dish is done, but you could finish it off with a handful of shredded spinach leaves, toasted sunflower seeds, and/or a knob of butter, but these are optional. Remove the bay leaves and cinnamon and serve as suggested in the introduction above.
Serves 6.

STUFFED BRINJALS RATATOUILLE

Plumped with vegetables and lentils, and blanketed with melting cheese, these brinjals make a super main course.

4 elongated brinjals (1 kg)
60 ml (¼ cup) sunflower oil
2 medium onions, finely chopped
3 cloves garlic, crushed
5 ml (1 tsp) mixed dried herbs
3 medium tomatoes (360 g), skinned and chopped
250 g baby marrows, pared and diced
75 ml (5 tbsp) chopped parsley
a little salt, pepper and sugar
125 ml (½ cup) vegetable stock or water
1 x 400 g can lentils, drained, or 300 ml cooked brown lentils
thinly sliced Mozzarella or other melting cheese
paprika and slivers of butter

Scrub brinjals, remove calyx and halve lengthwise. Score flesh in a diamond pattern, sprinkle with salt and stand for 30 minutes, then rinse and dry. Using a grapefruit knife, scoop out the flesh, leaving a firm shell.

Heat oil, add onions, garlic and herbs and, when softening, add tomatoes, baby marrows, parsley, seasoning, stock or water, and brinjal flesh. Cover and simmer for about 15 minutes, until soft, then mix in lentils.

Arrange brinjal shells close together in a large baking dish. Fill with stuffing, top generously with cheese, sprinkle with paprika and dot with butter. Pour a little water in at the side and bake, uncovered, at 180 °C for 30 minutes, then at 160 °C for 20 minutes, or until the brinjals are soft and the cheese is a melting, golden brown. Serves 8.

* This dish may be assembled in advance, ready for baking.

BEST BUDGET RICE AND LENTIL SALAD

Vegetarians need to combine grains and pulses in their main meals and that is why I have slotted this salad into the vegetarian, rather than the salad, section. Although so basic and budget, it's a terrific salad and enjoyed by non-vegetarians as well, who can be further wooed by adding the perfect accompaniment – a green salad tossed with fresh herbs and a creamy dressing.

250 ml (200 g) brown lentils, picked over and rinsed
250 ml (200 g) brown rice
2 leeks, thinly sliced and blanched
125 ml (½ cup) finely chopped parsley
2 sticks table celery, sliced
1 large red pepper, seeded and diced
75 ml (5 tbsp) toasted sunflower seeds
75 ml (5 tbsp) currants

DRESSING
150 ml (⅗ cup) sunflower oil
30 ml (2 tbsp) lemon juice
15 ml (1 tbsp) soy sauce
2 cloves garlic, crushed

Boil lentils and rice separately in salted water – the lentils will require 500 ml (2 cups) water, the rice a little more, and both should be done in about 50 minutes, with all the water absorbed. If not, drain before tipping into a large bowl.

Mix ingredients for dressing and pour over hot lentils and rice, toss to mix, then fork in remaining ingredients – do this gently so as not to mash up the lentils. Cover loosely and stand for 1–2 hours before serving. Serves 8.

To 'pick over' pulses before cooking, spread out and flick through to check for grit. Check chickpeas specially carefully.

CREAMY CHICKPEA, MUSHROOM AND APPLE CURRY

Those who complain that vegetarian meals take too long to prepare will welcome this recipe. The curry cooks in about 20 minutes flat, and the rice can be boiled at the same time. Serve with a bowl of thick yoghurt and a salad – the Tomato, Avocado and Coriander Salad (see page 55) makes a super accompaniment.

60 ml (¼ cup) sunflower oil
1 large onion, finely chopped
2 cloves garlic, crushed
20–25 ml (4–5 tsp) curry powder
5 ml (1 tsp) each ground cumin, ginger and turmeric
250 g white mushrooms, wiped and chopped
2 sweet apples, peeled and finely diced
20 ml (4 tsp) flour
250 ml (1 cup) milk
2 x 425 g cans chickpeas, undrained
15 ml (1 tbsp) tomato paste
10 ml (2 tsp) lemon juice
5 ml (1 tsp) each sugar and salt

Heat oil in a large frying pan, add onion and garlic and, when softening, add spices. Sizzle gently until fragrant, then add mushrooms and apples, and toss until golden – if mixture seems dry, add a little water. Sprinkle in the flour and, when absorbed, stir in milk, then add remaining ingredients, cover and simmer for about 20 minutes, stirring now and then, until thickened and creamy. Check seasoning.
Serves 6–8.

Fresh coriander has a flavour apart and is essential in Indian-style dishes. It is usually sold in little bunches and should be used when very fresh.

HARICOT BEANS WITH TOMATOES AND MUSHROOMS

A succulent, super vegetarian stew. Serve with baked potatoes, brown rice or pasta, and a green salad.

30 ml (2 tbsp) sunflower oil
a nut of butter
1 large onion, chopped
2 cloves garlic, crushed
1 red pepper, seeded and diced
5 ml (1 tsp) mixed dried herbs
1 x 400 g can tomatoes, chopped, plus juice
2 bay leaves
5 ml (1 tsp) sugar
125 ml (½ cup) vegetable stock or water
500–750 ml (360–540 g) cooked haricot beans*
a large handful of chopped parsley
250 g white or brown mushrooms, wiped and sliced
30 ml (2 tbsp) tomato sauce
30 ml (2 tbsp) soy sauce

Heat the oil and butter in a large, deep frying pan. Add the onion, garlic, red pepper and herbs, and sauté on low heat for a few minutes. Add the tomatoes, bay leaves, sugar and stock, cover and simmer very gently for 15 minutes, stirring occasionally to mash up the tomatoes. Add the remaining ingredients, mix lightly in order not to mash up the beans, then cover and simmer for about 15 minutes, until the mushrooms have softened and the sauce is chunky and thick.
Serves 6.

* To cook haricot beans, rinse the beans, soak in cold water overnight, drain and rinse again. Place in a large saucepan, cover with cold water, boil rapidly for 10 minutes, then cover and simmer until soft – for about 45 minutes. Add salt towards the end of the cooking period. Chickpeas and soya beans will take about 3 hours to cook.

STIR-FRIED VEGETABLES WITH APPLE JUICE AND GARLIC BUTTER

Almost any mixture of vegetables can be used to make a good stir-fry, but this one is delectably different. The mangetout add a gourmet touch, the apple juice adds a new flavour, and the finished dish is a cheerful riot of colours. This is a nutritious, main-course vegetarian dish, not an accompaniment.

45 ml (3 tbsp) sunflower oil
5 ml (1 tsp) dark sesame oil
1 large onion, sliced into thin rings
2 cloves garlic, crushed
200 g carrots, julienned
350 g baby marrows, pared and julienned
200 g white mushrooms, wiped and sliced
500 ml (125 g) lentil sprouts
125 g mangetout, topped and tailed
250 ml (1 cup) unsweetened apple juice
15 ml (1 tbsp) cornflour
30 ml (2 tbsp) soy sauce
toasted sesame seeds and pats of garlic butter* for topping

Heat the oils in a large wok or frying pan. If using a non-stick wok, follow the manufacturerer's instructions. Add the onion, garlic, carrots and baby marrows to the wok or pan, and toss over medium heat for about 5 minutes.

Add the mushrooms, sprouts and mangetout, and toss for a further 5 minutes or until everything is glistening and tender-crisp. Mix the apple juice, cornflour and soy sauce, add to the pan and stir until boiling and thickened.

Spoon into a large, heated serving dish, and sprinkle with sesame seeds. Serve ladled over brown rice, and top each serving with a pat of garlic butter.
Serves 4–5.

* To make garlic butter, mix 1 clove garlic, crushed, into 60 g creamed butter. Shape into a sausage, roll in waxed paper, and chill. Slice into thin rounds. If preferred, omit garlic and use fresh herbs such as parsley, chives, thyme, or whatever you have growing.

POTATOES STUFFED WITH SPINACH AND RICOTTA

A baked potato with sour cream is a popular last-ditch meal for many a vegetarian, but one that invariably becomes boring. This version requires extra time and ingredients, but it is so tasty that even meat-lovers will be happy – and so will the cook, as the potatoes can be completely assembled in advance. Serve with lightly fried mushrooms sauced with a little sour cream to add succulence, and steamed butternut for colour.

6–8 large baking potatoes
250 g frozen spinach, thawed
250 g Ricotta cheese
5 ml (1 tsp) salt
a little milled black pepper
6 spring onions, chopped
1 ml (¼ tsp) freshly grated nutmeg
Mozzarella or other melting cheese, thinly sliced
paprika

Scrub the potatoes, prick, rub with a little oil and bake at 200 °C until cooked.

When cool enough to handle, cut a horizontal slice off one side and scoop out most of the flesh, using a grapefruit spoon and leaving a firm shell. Arrange the potato skin shells in a large, shallow baking dish.

Cook the spinach, uncovered, until all the moisture has evaporated, and add to the potato flesh together with the Ricotta, seasoning, onions and nutmeg. Mash well, then spoon into the shells. As the mixture is dry (containing neither butter nor milk), it is possible to mound the filling really high to allow for maximum stuffing.

Top with Mozzarella cheese, dust with paprika and set aside if working ahead.

Heat through in the oven at 180 °C until the potatoes are piping hot and the cheese has melted and browned.

Serves 6–8.

ALMOND RISOTTO WITH SPINACH COUSCOUS

This unusual meal combines a surprising mixture of ingredients from a variety of cuisines. It is easy, despite the steps involved, and most delicious.

TOMATO AND AVOCADO RELISH
400 g tomatoes, diced small
30 ml (2 tbsp) olive oil
15 ml (1 tbsp) red wine vinegar
a little salt, sugar and milled black pepper
4 spring onions, chopped
15–30 ml (1–2 tbsp) tomato-based chilli sauce
1 large avocado, sliced
a sprinkling of garam masala

COUSCOUS WITH SPINACH
250 ml (180 g) couscous
250 ml (45 g) shredded spinach
1 ml (¼ tsp) grated nutmeg
a pinch of salt
250 ml (1 cup) boiling water

ALMOND RICE
45 ml (3 tbsp) sunflower oil
1 medium onion, chopped
2 cloves garlic, crushed
1 red pepper, seeded and diced
2 sticks table celery, plus leaves, chopped
5 ml (1 tsp) each ground coriander, ginger and cumin
250 ml (200 g) long-grain white rice
75 ml (5 tbsp) currants
500 ml (2 cups) hot vegetable stock or salted water
60 g slivered almonds, toasted
30 ml (2 tbsp) butter
4–6 fried or poached eggs

In a china serving bowl, mix all ingredients for the Tomato and Avocado Relish except avocado and masala, cover, and set aside.

Place couscous, spinach, nutmeg and salt in a bowl, pour boiling water over, stir to mix, then cover and set aside.

To make Almond Rice, heat oil in a large frying pan, add onion, garlic, pepper, celery and spices, toss for 1 minute, add rice and mix until coated. Add currants and stock, then cover and simmer for about 25 minutes, until liquid is absorbed.

Fork in prepared couscous, almonds and butter. Pile into a large, heated serving dish and top with eggs.

Top the Relish with avocado slices and garam masala, and serve it separately.
Serves 4–6.

POLENTA

A fine-grained, butter-yellow polenta meal is available at speciality shops and wholefood stores. It cooks to a much smoother texture than coarse-grained maize meal, but does require more water – see the packet for instructions.

For a savoury polenta, add parsley, garlic, grated Parmesan cheese and butter when cooked – see the next recipe.

CHEESY BAKED POLENTA

Just take a look at what has happened to stiff, old-fashioned maize meal porridge! It has been a staple food in Africa for centuries, and a traditional old favourite in Italy, however, it is not widely acclaimed elsewhere. Although it can be served plain or fried, and with meat, the following recipe, in which the polenta is flavoured with herbs and enriched with cheese and butter, makes a nourishing vegetarian meal if served with a fresh tomato or mushroom sauce and a salad. I have simplified the preparation as much as possible, but those not familiar with cooking maize meal should follow the instructions carefully. For polenta, it is very important that the meal should be cooked until really thick, and I find the following quantity of water used with coarse, yellow meal is spot on, but you might have to adjust it according to a different grade of meal. I also find that a double boiler is essential if you want to avoid on-going stirring and possible burning. Otherwise it is quite straightforward, really, and it's different, and fun.

400 ml (250 g) yellow maize meal
1 litre (4 cups) water
7 ml (1½ tsp) salt
15 ml (1 tbsp) sunflower oil
125 ml (½ cup) chopped parsley
2 cloves garlic, crushed
75 ml (5 tbsp) grated Parmesan cheese
30 ml (2 tbsp) butter
grated Cheddar or Mozzarella cheese for topping

Mix maize meal with half the water, stirring until smooth. Bring the remaining water, salt and oil to the boil in the top half of a large, deep double boiler, placed directly on the stove.

Slowly add the creamed meal, stirring all the time – use a long-handled spoon, as the mixture spatters furiously once boiling and easily burns your hand. Allow to bubble for a few minutes until smooth, then place on the base of the double boiler filled with boiling water, cover and simmer, stirring occasionally, for about at least 35 minutes, until very thick – you should be able to stand a spoon upright in the mixture without it falling over.

Stir in parsley, garlic, Parmesan cheese and butter, and turn into a lightly oiled, 25 cm square, ovenproof dish, spreading evenly to a thickness of about 2,5 cm. Leave until cold and firm, then cut into 12 squares, sprinkle with cheese, and bake at 180 °C for 30 minutes. Use a spatula to lift out the squares.
Serves 6.

* If serving a tomato sauce as an accompaniment, stir in plenty of chopped fresh basil towards the end of the cooking period.

FRESH VEGETABLE VINAIGRETTE

This is a fabulous salad. Bright, chunky and succulent, it makes a choice addition to any buffet, and the fact that the uncooked vegetables and the dressing are simply mixed and left in the refrigerator for 24 hours while their friendship develops is a bonus for any hostess. Serve the salad piled onto a large, lettuce-lined serving platter.

300 g well-trimmed cauliflower florets
½ (200 g) English cucumber
300 g baby marrows, pared and julienned
200 g white mushrooms, wiped and thinly sliced
4 spring onions, chopped
4 medium carrots, thinly julienned
chopped fresh tarragon and/or toasted sunflower seeds to garnish

DRESSING
200 ml (⅘ cup) sunflower oil (or half olive, half sunflower)
30 ml (2 tbsp) tarragon vinegar
30 ml (2 tbsp) lemon juice
5 ml (1 tsp) salt
10 ml (2 tsp) sugar
a few tufts of parsley
5 ml (1 tsp) dried tarragon

Slice cauliflower into thin pieces, soak briefly in salt water to remove any grit, then rinse and pat dry with kitchen paper.
Pare the cucumber, halve lengthwise, flick out the seeds and slice into thin strips.
Mix all the vegetables in a very large, shallow glass or pottery platter – do not use a deep bowl as the vegetables need to nestle in the dressing.
Place ingredients for dressing in a blender and pulse to mix. Pour over vegetables, toss well, then cover and refrigerate for 24 hours, removing once or twice during that period to give them a good stir. Eventually most of the dressing will have been absorbed, leaving the vegetables slightly softened, juicy and flavoursome. Garnish with chopped tarragon and/or sunflower seeds.
Serves 8.

MUSHROOM AND BABY MARROW SALAD WITH A CREAMY DRESSING

For a double-quick salad, fold the uncooked vegetables into a one-step dressing. The following combination is super with anything, but particularly good as a contrast to hot curry.

250 g white mushrooms, wiped and thinly sliced
250 g baby marrows, pared and sliced wafer-thin
extra chopped fresh chives to garnish

DRESSING
90 ml (6 tbsp) sunflower oil
15 ml (1 tbsp) lemon juice
90 ml (6 tbsp) thick Bulgarian yoghurt
90 ml (6 tbsp) cultured sour cream
2 ml (½ tsp) salt
1 small clove garlic, crushed
a pinch of sugar
30 ml (2 tbsp) each chopped parsley and chives

Place the vegetables for salad in a large, shallow salad bowl.
To make the dressing, whisk together all the ingredients with a fork until creamy. Pour over the vegetables, then toss and fold gently until the mushroom and marrow slices are all coated with the dressing.
Cover, and refrigerate for about 1 hour. Sprinkle with chopped chives before serving.
Serves 8.

RICE AND BULGUR SALAD

Add a handful of bulgur to a straightforward rice salad for a magical combination.

Although the result is similar in appearance to minty tabbouleh, the flavour is quite different and, without the mint, less dominant, so it is altogether more versatile. Super with anything.

125 ml (70 g) bulgur
500 ml (250 g) cooked white or brown rice
4 spring onions, chopped
1 each red and yellow pepper, seeded and julienned
250 ml (about 90 g) mixed sprouts
90 ml (6 tbsp) sunflower seeds, lightly toasted
a large handful of chopped parsley
6–8 spinach leaves, finely shredded

DRESSING
90 ml (6 tbsp) sunflower oil
30 ml (2 tbsp) soy sauce
10 ml (2 tsp) honey
15 ml (1 tbsp) lemon juice

Soak bulgur for 45 minutes in cold water to cover generously. Drain in a sieve and squeeze out all the water with your hands. Tip into a large bowl and mix in the rice and remaining salad ingredients. Mix the ingredients for the dressing, and fork into the rice mixture. Cover, and stand for 1–2 hours, or refrigerate overnight. **Serves 6.**

> *Sunflower seeds are nourishing and crunchy, and are cheaper than nuts. They can, however, be 'dusty' and should therefore be rinsed, spread out on baking trays and dried out in a low oven. Allowing them to toast lightly will enhance the flavour.*

TOMATO, AVOCADO AND CORIANDER SALAD

The ultimate salad to serve with curries, and so much nicer than the regular mix of chopped tomato and onion.

The fresh coriander and a sprinkling of garam masala add an emphatic Eastern flavour to curry dishes – however, if you do not have fresh coriander, substitute fresh basil, omit the garam masala, and serve the salad with a dish of pasta instead.

800 g medium tomatoes, washed but unpeeled, and sliced into rings
4 leeks, thinly sliced and blanched
2 large avocados, sliced into crescents
salt and milled black pepper
garam masala for topping

DRESSING
125 ml (½ cup) sunflower oil
30 ml (2 tbsp) lemon juice
60 ml (4 tbsp) chopped fresh coriander leaves*
5 ml (1 tsp) sugar
1 clove garlic, crushed
2 ml (½ tsp) ground cumin

Layer tomatoes, leeks and avocado in a large, shallow salad dish, seasoning each layer as you go. Mix ingredients for dressing, pour over salad, cover and stand for 30 minutes. Sprinkle with masala and serve. **Serves 8–10.**

* Measure coriander loosely as it is a surprisingly assertive herb.

> *To remove the strident flavour of raw onions, leeks and fresh green peppers, pour boiling water over the sliced vegetables. Add a pinch of sugar, leave to stand for 5 minutes, drain and pat dry.*

A SALAD FOR ALL SEASONS

This recipe makes a perfect luncheon salad, a good brunch salad, even a nice starter salad. Jiggle with quantities and ingredients as you like. Serve in a beautiful, big bowl, make the dressing at least an hour in advance, and serve separately

torn lettuce and shredded
  spinach for 6 people
90 g mixed sprouts
250 g cauliflower florets,
  lightly cooked
250 g baby marrows, pared
  and coarsely grated
150 g white mushrooms,
  wiped and thinly sliced
150 g cheese, diced – try
  medium-fat Havarti or feta
3 hard-boiled eggs, chopped
a few rashers of bacon, fried,
  drained and crumbled
125 ml (60 g) toasted
  sunflower seeds or chopped
  walnuts

ITALIAN DRESSING
250 ml (1 cup) sunflower or
  olive oil, or a mixture of both
30 ml (2 tbsp) lemon juice
30 ml (2 tbsp) Balsamic
  vinegar
a few tufts of parsley
1 clove garlic, chopped
5 ml (1 tsp) each dried basil
  and origanum
5 ml (1 tsp) honey
a pinch of salt

Toss together all the ingredients for the salad. Place the ingredients for the dressing in a blender and pulse until combined, then blend again just before serving, or make ahead and keep refrigerated in a glass jar.
Serves 6.

HINT
I also like to add a bouquet of fresh herbs to the salad – perennials such as marjoram, thyme and lemon thyme are lovely and always available.

MEDITERRANEAN THREE-BEAN SALAD

Three-Bean Salad is a well-known evergreen, but I have always been puzzled by the regular recipes which require a large dose of vinegar which then has to be tempered with an awful lot of sugar, which seems quite out of place in a salad, and also leaves the beans swamped in dressing. The following version is quite different. Fresh green beans replace the canned product, honey replaces the sugar, just enough red wine vinegar and oil are used for succulence, and the origanum and garnish provide a new, Continental flavour. Make the day before, and serve at a buffet lunch or barbecue, or with pita breads for lunch.

300 g fresh green beans,
  trimmed and sliced
1 large onion, sliced into
  thin rings
1 x 410 g can beans in tomato
  sauce, undrained
1 x 410 g can butter beans,
  drained
1 red pepper, seeded and diced
75 ml (5 tbsp) red wine vinegar
30 ml (2 tbsp) honey
125 ml (½ cup) sunflower oil
2 cloves garlic, crushed
5 ml (1 tsp) dried origanum
cubed feta cheese and black
  olives to garnish

Cook fresh beans in a little salted water and, just before end of the cooking period, place onion rings on the top to steam and take the edge off the raw bite.
  Drain, turn into a large, shallow glass bowl (a 23 cm pie dish is perfect), and mix in the canned beans and red pepper.
  Place all the remaining ingredients in a saucepan, heat and bubble gently for a few minutes while stirring. Pour over the beans, toss to mix, cool, cover and refrigerate overnight. Garnish with feta cheese and olives before serving.
Serves 8.

MARINATED MUSHROOMS

1
1 medium onion sliced into thin rings
1–2 cloves garlic, crushed
75 ml (5 tbsp) sunflower oil
30 ml (2 tbsp) lemon juice
30 ml (2 tbsp) white wine
60 ml (¼ cup) water
2 ml (½ tsp) each salt and sugar
30 ml (2 tbsp) chopped parsley
a few black peppercorns
2 bay leaves
several sprigs of fresh thyme
400 g tiny button mushrooms, wiped

Place all ingredients, except mushrooms, in a large frying pan and bring to the boil. Add mushrooms, reduce heat, cover and simmer very gently for 3–4 minutes. Transfer everything to a shallow glass dish which will allow mushrooms to lie in the liquid, cool, cover and refrigerate overnight. Remove sprigs of thyme, bay leaves and peppercorns before serving.
Serves 6–8 as a salad.

2
500 g white mushrooms, wiped
250 ml (1 cup) sunflower oil
60 ml (¼ cup) lemon juice
10 ml (2 tsp) chopped rosemary leaves
10 ml (2 tsp) Dijon mustard
2 ml (½ tsp) salt
a few tufts of parsley
2 spring onions, chopped
2 cloves garlic, chopped
10 ml (2 tsp) honey

Chop the mushrooms into large chunks and place in a shallow, glass dish. Place the remaining ingredients in a blender, blend well, pour over the mushrooms, toss until coated, then cover and refrigerate overnight.
Serves 6–8.

SESAME STIR-FRIED SALAD

A garden of vegetables is tucked into this versatile salad, which may be served as a first course with Sesame and Garlic Toasts (see page 10), or as the best thing that ever happened to cold chicken, beef or pork.

125 ml (½ cup) sunflower oil
7 ml (1½ tsp) dark sesame oil
2 cloves garlic, crushed
250 g baby marrows, pared and julienned
180 g broccoli, trimmed and sliced lengthwise
4 medium (180 g) carrots, julienned
200 g white mushrooms, wiped and sliced
2 ml (½ tsp) ground ginger
15 ml (1 tbsp) honey
45 ml (3 tbsp) soy sauce
30 ml (2 tbsp) lemon juice
60 ml (¼ cup) water
toasted sesame seeds to garnish

Use a wok or very large frying pan. Heat oils and garlic. Add marrows, broccoli and carrots, and toss until just beginning to soften, then mix in mushrooms. Sprinkle with ginger, drizzle with honey, then add remaining ingredients and toss until vegetables are tender, shiny and succulent – not limp. Turn vegetables and juices into a large, shallow serving dish, cover loosely and leave to cool. Sprinkle with sesame seeds before serving.
Serves 6–8.

Toasting brings out the flavour of sesame seeds – spread out on a baking tray and place in a low oven until lightly browned, or toast in a non-stick frying pan on low heat. Shake frequently, as they burn easily.

CLASSIC GREEN SALAD WITH FRESH HERBS

Once upon a time the word 'salads' brought visions of beetroot in vinegar, potatoes in sweet yellow mayonnaise, grated carrots. These days, salad-making is a very studied business: 'baby' vegetables, bacon, blue cheese, Balsamic vinegar, walnut oil. It all becomes very busy and expensive and one forgets the perfection of simple, crisp greens with a dressing of fresh herbs. This is a reminder.

a mixture of lettuce leaves (butter, oak leaf, cos, iceberg)
a mixture of sprouts
1 avocado, sliced

DRESSING
125 ml (½ cup) sunflower oil
45 ml (3 tbsp) lemon juice
30 ml (2 tbsp) chopped parsley
60 ml (4 tbsp) chopped fresh herbs*
1 clove garlic, crushed
2–3 slim spring onions, chopped
2 ml (½ tsp) sugar

Rinse and dry the salad leaves and sprouts – the total weight should be about 300 g or enough for 6 people. Wrap and chill.

Mix all the ingredients for the dressing and pour into a salad bowl. At serving time, add the greens to the dressing in the salad bowl, and toss everything together until glistening, including the avocado.

Serve as is, or add either walnuts or crispy croûtons for crunch.
Serves 6.

* Use fresh chives, tarragon, marjoram or sage.

NOTE
More and more cooks are cutting down on salt, and it certainly is not essential in a well-flavoured dressing.

CAULIFLOWER, LEEK AND RADISH SALAD

A lightly spiced salad which is super with curries.

1 large cauliflower
4 leeks, sliced
1 red pepper, seeded and diced
6 radishes (90 g), trimmed and thinly sliced
a pinch of garam masala and/or chopped hard-boiled eggs to garnish

DRESSING
125 ml (½ cup) sunflower oil
30 ml (2 tbsp) lemon juice
30 ml (2 tbsp) each chopped parsley and chives
2 cloves garlic, crushed
5 ml (1 tsp) ground cumin

First mix the ingredients for the dressing, so that it is ready to pour over the hot cauliflower.

Divide the cauliflower into small florets – you should have 600 g, with all the thick stems removed. Poach, together with the leeks, in a little salted water until just tender – be careful not to overcook. Drain, but do not refresh.

Place in a large, shallow salad dish, and gently mix in red pepper, radishes and dressing. Cover loosely and stand for 1–2 hours.

If using eggs, chop the whites finely and grate the yolks, and use to garnish the salad, then sprinkle garam masala over the top.
Serves 6–8.

When using fresh herbs, strip the leaves by pulling downwards, opposite to the direction of growth, and discard the stalks.

LEBANESE TABBOULEH

Tabbouleh is such an easy grain salad and so good that it need not be reserved for Middle Eastern meals. With its minty flavour it is great with lamb or grilled kebabs, but if you wish to serve it traditionally, use it as a stuffing for pita breads or as a starter on a platter of meze. There are many versions, all basically similar, and this is my favourite.

250 ml (180 g) bulgur*
½ bunch of spring onions, including some green tops, chopped
125 ml (½ cup) finely chopped parsley
30 ml (2 tbsp) finely chopped mint leaves
2 medium tomatoes, finely chopped
1 small red pepper, seeded and diced
45 ml (3 tbsp) currants
60 ml (¼ cup) olive oil (or half sunflower, half olive)
1 clove garlic, crushed
2 ml (½ tsp) ground cumin
30 ml (2 tbsp) lemon juice
salt and milled black pepper
toasted sunflower seeds to garnish

Pour plenty of cold water over bulgur in a bowl and leave to stand for about 45 minutes. Tip into a sieve and squeeze out as much moisture as possible, then turn into a large bowl. Add onions, parsley, mint, tomatoes, red pepper and currants, and toss to mix. Whisk together oil, garlic, cumin and lemon juice, pour over salad and toss with a fork to combine. Season, cover, and stand for about 2 hours to develop flavours. (May also be refrigerated overnight, in which case do not add tomatoes until just before serving.) Mound on a platter and scatter with sunflower seeds. **Serves 4.**

* Bulgur is sometimes called crushed wheat and is sold in wholefood stores. Cracked wheat cannot be substituted.

POTATO AND CORN SALAD WITH MUSTARD DRESSING

Despite the preference these days for serving grain salads, there is still a niche for cold, well-dressed potatoes, and this snappy version is quite different from the old-fashioned, waxy mixture in cooked salad cream.

500 g small, new potatoes, well scrubbed and halved
5 ml (1 tsp) dried tarragon
30 ml (2 tbsp) garlicky French dressing
1 x 410 g can whole kernel corn, well-drained
4–6 spring onions, chopped
60 ml (¼ cup) mayonnaise
60 ml (¼ cup) cultured sour cream
15 ml (1 tbsp) wholegrain mustard
5 ml (1 tsp) Dijon mustard
5 ml (1 tsp) honey
fresh tarragon or chopped parsley to garnish

Boil potatoes in salted water with tarragon, until cooked. Drain, shake dry, place in a shallow salad bowl, pour dressing over potatoes, and shake to coat. Mix in corn and onions, and leave until cold and dressing has been absorbed. Mix remaining ingredients, then fold into salad. Sprinkle with fresh tarragon or chopped parsley, and serve. **Serves 6.**

Whole milk Bulgarian yoghurt is much less tart and sharp than low-fat yoghurt, and this is the kind I use when toning down mayonnaise.

CURRIED RICE, APPLE AND WALNUT SALAD

A thumpingly good combination of spicy rice and crunchy good things. Try serving it with a creamy chicken salad, or with any dish that requires a perky rice salad as a mate.

250 ml (200 g) brown or white rice
75 ml (5 tbsp) sunflower oil
2 slim leeks, very thinly sliced
2 cloves garlic, crushed
15 ml (1 tbsp) curry powder
5 ml (1 tsp) each ground cumin and turmeric
60 g walnuts, coarsely chopped
30 ml (2 tbsp) lemon juice
30 ml (2 tbsp) chutney
1 large carrot, coarsely grated
1 sweet apple, peeled and coarsely grated
75 ml (5 tbsp) seedless raisins
60 ml (4 tbsp) chopped parsley

Boil the rice in salted water (or stock for added flavour) until dry and fluffy – this is important, or your salad will be mushy. Keep warm in a colander over simmering water. Heat the oil, add the leeks, garlic, spices and walnuts, and toss until the leeks have softened and the spices are aromatic. Remove from the stove and stir in the lemon juice and chutney. Place the rice in a bowl, fork in the fried mixture, then add the remaining ingredients, tossing until combined. Cover loosely and stand for about 1 hour before serving, or refrigerate.
Serves 5–6.

Always use FRESH lemon juice. If you pour boiling water over the lemon before squeezing, it should yield extra juice.

RICE SALAD WITH MUSHROOMS AND SPROUTS

A flop-proof favourite, plump with mushrooms, crunchy with sprouts and great with chicken salads – the flavours complement Pineapple-Sesame Chicken Salad (see page 41) especially well.

60 ml (¼ cup) sunflower oil
2 onions, sliced into thin rings
2 sticks table celery, plus some leaves, chopped
2 cloves garlic, crushed
400 ml (320 g) long-grain white rice
250 g brown mushrooms, wiped and chopped
800 ml (3⅕ cups) chicken stock
45 ml (3 tbsp) sherry
30 ml (2 tbsp) soy sauce
90 ml (6 tbsp) chopped parsley
375 ml (90 g) lentil sprouts
a nut of butter

Heat oil in a large frying pan. Add onions, celery and garlic, and toss to separate onion rings. When softening, reduce heat, add rice, stir briefly, and then add mushrooms. Toss until aromatic, then add stock, sherry and soy sauce. Cover and simmer on very low heat for 20–25 minutes, until rice is cooked but still moist and shiny. Remove from stove and fork in parsley, sprouts and butter. Tip into a bowl and cool. If working ahead, cover and chill, but remove from the refrigerator 30 minutes before serving.
Serves 8.

BASIC BLENDER DRESSING
Blend together 500 ml (2 cups) sunflower oil, 100 ml (⅖ cup) lemon juice, 5 ml (1 tsp) mustard powder, a pinch of salt, 1–2 cloves chopped garlic, 2 chopped spring onions and a few tufts of parsley.
Makes 600 ml (2⅖ cups)

RICE, LENTIL AND MUSHROOM SALAD

A perennially popular, wholesome luncheon salad. For a complete vegetarian meal, garnish as suggested and serve with a home-made wholewheat loaf.

200 ml (160 g) brown rice
200 ml (160 g) brown lentils, picked over and rinsed*
75 ml (5 tbsp) sunflower oil
2 leeks, sliced
1 each green and red pepper, seeded and julienned
250 g brown mushrooms, wiped and sliced
2 sprigs fresh rosemary
90 ml (6 tbsp) chopped parsley
45 ml (3 tbsp) soy sauce
30 ml (2 tbsp) sweet sherry
5 ml (1 tsp) sugar

TOPPING
yoghurt
chopped walnuts
hard-boiled eggs and sliced avocados to garnish

Place the rice and lentils in a heavy saucepan, first smearing the base with a slick of oil to prevent sticking. Add 900 ml (3⅗ cups) water and a little salt, bring to the boil, then cover and cook on low heat for about 45 minutes, until tender. The liquid should be absorbed, but drain if necessary.

Meanwhile, heat 60 ml (¼ cup) oil and stir-fry leeks and peppers. When they are softening, add mushrooms and rosemary. Cook over low heat until just tender. Remove from heat, stir in parsley and remove rosemary. Mix soy sauce, sherry, sugar and remaining oil, and add to the mushroom mixture.

Tip cooked rice and lentils into a large bowl. Fork in vegetable mixture. Cool, then cover and stand for about 2 hours, or refrigerate if working ahead, but allow to come to room temperature before serving. Drizzle with yoghurt and walnuts, and surround with hard-boiled eggs and avocado slices.
Serves 4–6.

* For finest flavour, use large, brown or khaki-coloured lentils, which are used for sprouting and are available from wholefood stores: 200 ml (4/5 cup) of these lentils equals 140 g.

ONE-STEP RATATOUILLE

Simply mix, bake, and serve hot or cold – this dish is such a pleasure. It is also a particularly quick version of the Provencale-style dish, except for the brinjals which, in this case, really have to be dégorged. Being neither fried nor grilled, those juices are going to go straight into the 'stew' and, if not dégorged, will add a bitter flavour.

800 g brinjals, cubed and dégorged
1 x 400 g can tomatoes, finely chopped, plus juice
125 ml (½ cup) olive oil
125 ml (½ cup) water
400 g baby marrows, pared and thinly sliced
2 leeks, sliced
4 cloves garlic, crushed
5 ml (1 tsp) dried origanum
1 ml (¼ tsp) dried thyme
10 ml (2 tsp) sugar
black olives to garnish

Place ingredients in a large baking dish and toss until everything is well acquainted. Cover securely and bake at 160 °C for about 1 hour until soft and juicy – remove from oven and stir once during the baking period, being careful not to mash the vegetables. Check the seasoning before serving – you may wish to add a pinch of salt – and garnish with black olives.
Serves 8–10.

MUSHROOMS AND MARROWS IN CREAM

If you're serving grilled steak or fish and need a really easy, creamy accompaniment, try this mix-and-bake recipe. It may be assembled in advance and baked when wanted – the result is a delicately flavoured and succulent side-dish.

500 g button mushrooms, wiped and halved
3 leeks, thinly sliced
2 large yellow peppers, seeded and chopped
400 g baby marrows, pared and very thinly sliced
180 ml (¾ cup) cultured sour cream
15 ml (1 tbsp) cornflour
20 ml (4 tsp) soy sauce
30 ml (2 tbsp) medium-dry sherry
30 ml (2 tbsp) water
2 cloves garlic, crushed
1 ml (¼ tsp) dried thyme
snipped garlic chives to garnish

Combine vegetables in a large mixing bowl. Stir together remaining ingredients, add to vegetables and toss until thoroughly moistened. Spoon into a large, oiled baking dish. If working ahead, cover and set aside at this stage. Bake, covered, at 180 °C for 30 minutes. Garnish.
Serves 8.

HONEYED GINGER CARROTS

It is amazing how easily the common old carrot can be elevated to take a proud place at a good dinner. These are particularly good with pork.

400 g carrots, julienned
30 ml (2 tbsp) butter
125 ml (½ cup) chicken stock or water
5 ml (1 tsp) ground ginger
15 ml (1 tbsp) honey
2 ml (½ tsp) salt
60 ml (4 tbsp) chopped parsley

Place all ingredients, except parsley, in a wide-based frying pan, bring to the boil, and then simmer, covered, for 3–4 minutes, until just tender. Uncover, increase heat, and shake pan until liquid has evaporated and carrots are glazed. Stir in parsley and serve.
Serves 4–5.

VEGETABLES AND GRAINS

GREEN BEANS AND CORN WITH CUMIN-SESAME BUTTER

Add a can of whole golden corn to plain green beans, gloss with lightly spiced butter, and you have a cheerful vegetable dish to grace either curries or chicken.

300 g green beans, trimmed and sliced diagonally
1 medium onion, sliced into thin rings
1 x 410 g can whole corn kernels, drained

SPICED BUTTER
30 ml (2 tbsp) butter
5 ml (1 tsp) ground cumin
1 clove garlic, crushed
15 ml (1 tbsp) toasted sesame seeds

First make spiced butter: mash butter with cumin and garlic, mix in seeds and set aside. Cook beans and onion in a little salted water until just tender.

Drain if necessary, return to saucepan, add corn and heat through, then add spiced butter and toss until melted.

Check seasoning – you might want to add a pinch of salt and/or sugar – then turn into a heated serving dish.
Serves 6.

When it comes to dégorging brinjals, some cooks do, and some don't. I think it is essential, unless the brinjals are really small. Medium to large brinjals can add a bitter flavour and extra juices to a dish.

To dégorge, wash the brinjals well, remove calyx, and slice or cube brinjal. Place in a colander, sprinkle generously with salt, leave for at least 30 minutes, rinse well, and pat dry with a paper towel.

BAKED SPICED BUTTERNUT SQUASH

A most unusual way of serving butternuts – cut into fat round discs, dusted with spices and dunked into sesame seeds. To make the discs, buy butternuts that are elongated as only the long, seedless ends are used. If time is short, make Orange Baked Butternut (see box).

2 large butternuts
5 ml (1 tsp) each salt, ground cinnamon, ginger and cumin
melted butter
90 ml (6 tbsp) sesame seeds
extra butter

Slice off the bulbous ends of butternuts, so that you are left with two long, solid cylinders. Peel and slice into 2 cm thick discs – you should have 10 discs with a total weight of 900 g. Mix salt and spices on a flat plate. Brush each slice of butternut with melted butter, press both sides into spices, then coat with sesame seeds, pressing on firmly.

Cover base of a large baking dish with baking paper and arrange butternut slices in the dish, not touching. If working ahead, set aside now.

Bake uncovered at 180 °C for about 1 hour or until soft. Top each slice with a blob of extra butter and return to oven to melt.
Serves 10.

ORANGE BAKED BUTTERNUT
Peel and cube 600 g butternut flesh, place in large baking dish. Mix 250 ml (1 cup) fresh orange juice, 30 ml (2 tbsp) butter, 30 ml (2 tbsp) soft brown sugar, 5 ml (1 tsp) ground ginger and 2 ml (½ tsp) each ground cinnamon, cumin and salt. Bring to boil, stirring, then pour over butternut, cover and bake.
Serves 4–5.

CAULIFLOWER WITH A CREAMY LEMON DRESSING

Instead of separating a cauliflower into florets, introduce a touch of style by cooking it whole and blanketing it with a sauce. The obvious saucy choices are Hollandaise or a cheesy Mornay. The first is tricky, and the second is old hat, while the following dressing – equally rich and tasty – is mixed in minutes.

1 medium to large cauliflower
fresh lemon juice for sprinkling
paprika for sprinkling

DRESSING
125 ml (½ cup) mayonnaise
125 ml (½ cup) cultured sour cream
30 ml (2 tbsp) lemon juice
30 ml (2 tbsp) finely chopped chives

Cut the thick stem off the cauliflower and pierce smaller stems with a sharp knife (alternatively, cut into large, single-serving clumps). Trimmed weight should be about 800 g. Soak briefly in salted water to remove any grit, then rinse well, sprinkle top with lemon juice and cook, stem down, in salted water until tender. Drain, place on a serving dish and keep warm.

Mix ingredients for dressing in the top of a double boiler and stir over simmering water until hot. For a sharper lemon flavour, add a little finely grated lemon rind. Pour over cauliflower, dust with paprika, and serve.
Serves 8.

Vegetables such as carrots, potatoes and baby marrows vary so much in size that weights have been specified where it is essential to use a certain quantity for the success of a recipe.

BAKED NEW POTATOES WITH ONIONS AND GARLIC

A delightful change from potatoes just tossed in parsley butter.

12 pickling onions
500 g new potatoes, scrubbed
8–10 cloves garlic, unpeeled
2 ml (½ tsp) salt
45 ml (3 tbsp) olive oil
15 ml (1 tbsp) butter
15 ml (1 tbsp) chopped fresh rosemary leaves

Place onions in a saucepan, cover with cold water, bring to the boil and cook for 5 minutes. Drain, nick off the base and slip off the skins. Arrange potatoes in a baking dish in a single layer, to fit quite closely. Tuck in onions and garlic. Sprinkle with salt. Melt oil and butter with rosemary, pour over and toss until shiny. Bake, covered, at 200 °C for 30 minutes or until potatoes are cooked and just starting to brown.
Serves 6.

MUSTARD CREAM
3 eggs
45 ml (3 tbsp) mustard powder
45 ml (3 tbsp) white wine vinegar
15 ml (1 tbsp) honey
a little salt
125 ml (½ cup) sunflower oil

Put all ingredients except oil into a double boiler and stir briskly over simmering water until smooth and very thick. Remove from heat, slowly whisk in oil, return to the stove and whisk for a few more minutes. Cool and store in a covered glass jar in the refrigerator. Add herbs if liked, or thin with buttermilk for a salad cream. Serve with cold roast beef.

BROWN RICE AND VEGETABLE BAKE

Containing a bumper crop of bright ingredients, this dish side-steps the need to cook rice and vegetables separately, and may conveniently be baked along with the main course. It makes a great accompaniment to anything – fish, meat or fowl – or serve it with a soya bean or chickpea casserole as a complete vegetarian meal.

60 ml (¼ cup) sunflower oil
1 medium onion, chopped
2 cloves garlic, crushed
1 each large red and green pepper, seeded and diced
375 ml (300 g) brown rice
200 g brown mushrooms, wiped and chopped
750 ml (3 cups) water
45 ml (3 tbsp) soy sauce
1 x 410 g can whole corn kernels, drained
a handful of chopped parsley
30 ml (2 tbsp) butter

Heat oil, add onion, garlic and peppers, and sauté briefly. Add rice and mushrooms, and toss until glistening. Add water and soy sauce, stir to mix, then turn into a 30 x 20 cm baking dish, spreading out evenly. Cover securely and bake at 160 °C for 1 hour, by which time the rice should be tender and the liquid absorbed. Fork in corn kernels, parsley and butter, and return to the oven briefly to heat through.
Serves 8.

When preparing green, red or yellow peppers, remove the seeds as well as the membranes or inner ribs before using.

FRAGRANT COUSCOUS

Couscous, a cereal made from semolina, is widely used in North Africa. Carelessly prepared, it can be lumpy and stodgy. Carefully treated, it makes an exotic change from rice and other cereals; the following recipe requires only 10 minutes to assemble from start to finish.

250 ml (180 g) couscous*
300 ml (1⅕ cups) salted, boiling water
30 ml (2 tbsp) butter
15 ml (1 tbsp) sunflower oil
5 ml (1 tsp) each ground cumin, turmeric and coriander
30 ml (2 tbsp) chopped parsley

Place couscous in a bowl, pour boiling water over, and stand for 5 minutes until water is absorbed. Heat butter and oil until melted, add spices and allow to bubble for a minute to mellow the flavours. Add to couscous, together with parsley, and then use a fork to break up the lumps – using quick, vigorous movements this will take about 1 minute. Spoon into a lightly buttered dish, cover and heat through in the oven at 160 °C.
Serves 4–5.

* Different brands of couscous may require varying methods of preparation and quantities of water – check instructions on the packet before adding the spices.

To make a fragrant couscous salad, omit the butter when 'cooking' the spices and use 60 ml (¼ cup) sunflower oil instead. Fork in a dash of lemon juice when adding the parsley, cover loosely and cool. Garnish with cashews or other toasted nuts.

CHEESECAKE POTS

This is a novel way of serving a 'cheesecake'. By omitting the crust you save on preparation time and quite a few kilojoules, and the cheesecake mixture (quickly blended in a processor) is set in individual ramekins. Once unmoulded they are lusciously decorated, with a drizzle of fruity coulis to tone down the decadence.

STRAWBERRY POTS
A light version, without egg yolks.

250 g strawberries, rinsed and hulled
90 ml (6 tbsp) castor sugar
250 g smooth, low-fat cottage cheese
12 ml (2½ tsp) gelatine
60 ml (¼ cup) water
125 ml (½ cup) cream
a few drops of vanilla essence
2 egg whites
extra whipped cream and strawberries to decorate
strawberry coulis

Slice strawberries and place in a processor fitted with the metal blade. Add half the sugar and stand for 10 minutes to draw the juices. Add cottage cheese and then pulse just until smoothly combined. Do not purée the strawberries to a mush – the mixture should be pale pink and flecked with little bits of berries. Turn into a large bowl.
  Sponge gelatine in water, dissolve over low heat, and slowly stir into cheese mixture. Fold in cream whipped with vanilla. Whisk egg whites until stiff, then gradually whisk in remaining 45 ml (3 tbsp) sugar to make a glossy meringue mixture. Fold the meringue into the cheese mixture gently but thoroughly.
  Pour into 8–10 rinsed ramekins or moulds and refrigerate until set. Unmould onto individual serving plates and decorate with whipped cream and strawberries, and flank with coulis.
Serves 8–10.

COULIS
This is simply puréed fruit, fresh or cooked, plain or sweetened. If the fruit is too firm to purée, a little juice may be added – orange goes well with mango, for example. A basic strawberry coulis is made by blending 250 g strawberries with 30 ml (2 tbsp) castor sugar. For a flavour perk, add 30 ml (2 tbsp) orange liqueur.
Makes about 350 ml (1⅖ cups).

When making cheesecakes set with gelatine, bring cottage or cream cheese to room temperature before using as warm gelatine will simply stiffen into threads if added to a cold mixture. And do not use eggs straight from the refrigerator as chilled egg whites will not whip.

CHERRY AMARETTO POTS
You can either pot this one, as in the previous recipe, or show off the colours by using fairly wide, tubby glasses or goblets. This is a stunning dessert that deserves to be beautifully presented.

500 g smooth, low-fat cottage cheese
125 ml (100 g) castor sugar
a pinch of salt
75–90 ml (5–6 tbsp) Amaretto liqueur
a few drops of vanilla essence
20 ml (4 tsp) gelatine
60 ml (¼ cup) water
250 ml (1 cup) cream, whipped
3 egg whites
extra 60 ml (4 tbsp) castor sugar

TOPPING
1 x 425 g can stoned black cherries, drained
2 ml (½ tsp) cornflour
60 ml (¼ cup) cherry syrup
whipped cream to decorate

Whisk or process cottage cheese, sugar, salt, liqueur and vanilla until smooth. Sponge gelatine in water and dissolve over low heat. Slowly drizzle gelatine into cheese mixture, whisking rapidly. Fold in cream. Whisk egg whites until stiff, then gradually add the extra sugar and whisk until very stiff. (If you do this first, and work quickly, you won't have to wash the beaters.) Fold into the cheese/cream mixture. Pour or spoon levelly into 10 pots or glasses and refrigerate until set.

To prepare topping, dry cherries with paper towels, and then carefully halve them, using a sharp knife. Arrange, rounded sides up, on top of each dessert. Slake cornflour with syrup, then boil for a few minutes until thick. Cool briefly, then use to glaze cherries, using a pastry brush. Pipe rosettes of cream in the open spaces and refrigerate until serving time.
Serves 10.

CHOCOLATE ORANGE POTS

100 g dark chocolate, broken into pieces
15 ml (1 tbsp) water
250 g smooth, low-fat cottage cheese
5 ml (1 tsp) finely grated orange rind
90 ml (6 tbsp) castor sugar
2 eggs, separated
60 ml (¼ cup) fresh orange juice
12 ml (2½ tsp) gelatine
125 ml (½ cup) cream
2 ml (½ tsp) vanilla essence
**extra whipped cream and chocolate curls to decorate
strawberry, mango or litchi coulis**

Grease a small container with a little butter, add the chocolate and water, and soften over low heat. Place the cheese, orange rind, sugar, egg yolks and melted chocolate in a processor fitted with the metal blade and process until smoothly combined. Turn into a large bowl, using a rubber spatula.

Pour the orange juice into the container in which the chocolate was melted, sprinkle on the gelatine, dissolve over low heat, then slowly stir into the chocolate mixture. Put aside briefly to start thickening while you set out the ramekins – you will need 6–8, rinsed out with water for easy unmoulding.

Whip the cream softly with the vanilla and fold into the chocolate mixture, followed by the egg whites, whisked with a pinch of salt. Fold over gently until combined, then pour into moulds and refrigerate until firm. Unmould and decorate with whipped cream and chocolate curls, and drizzle with coulis, just before serving.
Serves 6–8.

RAINBOW FRUIT SALAD AMARETTO

An elegant, refreshing finale.

1 x 410 g can pitted litchis, drained, syrup reserved
180 g ripe strawberries, halved, or quartered if large
3 kiwi fruit, peeled and sliced into rings
30 ml (2 tbsp) Amaretto liqueur

Snip litchis into slivers, then combine with the other fruit in a glass bowl. Pour reserved syrup – you should have just under 200 ml (⁴⁄₅ cup) – into a small saucepan and boil on high heat until reduced to 60 ml (¼ cup) and just starting to turn a light caramel colour. Remove from stove and add liqueur, then pour over fruit. Mix in carefully, so as not to break up the kiwi slices, then cool, cover and refrigerate for at least 2 hours.
Serves 4–6.

ARABIAN FRUIT SALAD WITH HONEYED CREAM

A pot-pourri of fresh fruit, dates, ginger and spices – this is much more exciting than plain fruit salad, but just as easy to prepare.

1 small pineapple, sliced into rings
2 large oranges, peeled and pith removed
2 large bananas, sliced
lemon juice
1 papino, peeled, seeded and diced (400 g flesh)
45 ml (3 tbsp) finely chopped preserved ginger
125 g pitted dates, chopped
10 ml (2 tsp) finely grated orange rind
60 ml (4 tbsp) castor sugar
250 ml (1 cup) cultured sour cream*
30 ml (2 tbsp) honey
1 ml (¼ tsp) ground cinnamon
toasted desiccated coconut to garnish

Remove the core from the pineapple rings and dice the flesh. Slice the oranges into thin rings and again into quarters. Toss the bananas with a little lemon juice. Mix the prepared fruits with the papino, ginger, dates and orange rind in a large glass bowl – use one that is wide-based rather than sloping. Sprinkle with the castor sugar, cover, and refrigerate for up to 3 hours.
 Stir together the sour cream, honey and cinnamon, cover, and refrigerate. Just before serving, swirl the cream mixture through the fruit and sprinkle the coconut over the top.
Serves 8–10.

* Use half sour cream with half thick Bulgarian yoghurt for a less rich mixture.

LITCHI AND GINGER CHEESECAKE

Exotic litchis perfectly complement the gingery, creamy filling in this cheesecake, quickly mixed in a processor.

FILLING
250 g smooth, low-fat cottage cheese
250 g cream cheese
125 ml (100 g) castor sugar
2 eggs, separated
30 ml (2 tbsp) finely chopped preserved ginger
5 ml (1 tsp) vanilla essence
1 x 410 g can pitted litchis, drained and syrup reserved
20 ml (4 tsp) gelatine
125 ml (½ cup) cream, whipped
whipped cream and toasted almonds to decorate
2 ml (½ tsp) cornflour slaked with 45 ml (3 tbsp) reserved syrup to glaze

Use your favourite biscuit crumb recipe to line a greased, 20 cm pie dish. Chill.

Place the cheese, sugar, egg yolks, ginger and vanilla in a processor fitted with the metal blade and process to a smooth mixture, with the ginger reduced to thin slivers. Spoon into a large mixing bowl. Pour 125 ml (½ cup) reserved litchi syrup into a small container, sprinkle the gelatine on top, then dissolve over low heat. Slowly stir into the creamed mixture and then chill briefly until just thickening. Fold in the cream, and then the egg whites, stiffly whisked with a pinch of salt. Pour onto the prepared crust and chill until set.

Halve the litchis, pat dry, and arrange, rounded sides up, over the top of the cheesecake. Boil up the cornflour slaked with reserved litchi syrup for the glaze until clear, and then paint the litchis. Refrigerate before serving.
Serves 8.

MUESLI APPLE CRUMBLE

This is quite different from a regular apple crumble. The wholesome topping of muesli, sunflower oil, nuts and spices is remarkably delicious, while the flavour of the apples is enhanced with honey and ginger. Serve this sweetly nostalgic dessert with softly whipped cream flavoured with a tot of brandy, or with ice cream, or plain yoghurt.

1 x 765 g can unsweetened pie apples*
15–30 ml (1–2 tbsp) chopped preserved ginger
60 ml (4 tbsp) seedless raisins
5 ml (1 tsp) ground cinnamon
30 ml (2 tbsp) honey
60 ml (4 tbsp) golden brown sugar
125 ml (½ cup) hot water

CRUMBLE
250 ml (110 g) unsweetened muesli
125 ml (60 g) self-raising flour
30 g pecan nuts, chopped
5 ml (1 tsp) ground cinnamon
90 ml (6 tbsp) golden brown sugar
125 ml (½ cup) sunflower oil

Chop apples, spoon into a deep, lightly buttered 20 cm pie dish, mix in ginger, then sprinkle with raisins and cinnamon. Dissolve honey and sugar in the hot water and pour over apples.

To make crumble, mix all dry ingredients, then stir in oil, combining thoroughly. Cover the apples with the crumble, and bake in the oven at 180 °C for 30 minutes, until browned and bubbling. Serve warm, or set aside and reheat briefly in a low oven before serving.
Serves 6–8.

* Use top-grade apples that are tightly packed, without juice.

TIPSY STRAWBERRIES WITH CLOVE-SCENTED CREAM

Macerated strawberries, infused cream and a sprinkling of milled black pepper add up to a perfectly groomed ending to the finest dinner party. Preparation is do-ahead and spectacularly simple.

750 g ripe strawberries, hulled, rinsed and sliced
125 ml (65 g) icing sugar
1 ml (¼ tsp) ground cinnamon
60 ml (¼ cup) orange liqueur
30 ml (2 tbsp) brandy

SCENTED CREAM
250 ml (1 cup) cream
12 cloves
4 x 3 cm strips orange peel
30 ml (2 tbsp) sifted icing sugar
a few drops of vanilla essence

Place the strawberries in a large, shallow glass bowl. Sift icing sugar and cinnamon over the strawberries. Add liqueur and brandy. Shake gently until no trace of icing sugar remains, then cover and chill in the refrigerator for up to 24 hours.
  To make cream, rinse a small saucepan with water (to prevent burning), add cream, cloves and orange peel, and slowly bring to scalding point on very low heat. Cool, then pour into a glass container, cover, and chill. Just before serving the dessert, remove the cloves and orange peel from the cream, add the sugar and vanilla, whip until floppy, and serve with the berries. Pass a pepper mill at the table for guests to try this novel finishing touch.
Serves 6.

When using honey in a recipe, choose a pale, thin variety as a dark honey could have too pronounced a flavour.

POACHED ORANGES IN LIQUEUR

Sweet and slightly tipsy, these succulent orange halves may be served refreshingly plain, or with ice cream, crème fraîche or softly whipped cream. This recipe can easily be doubled.

4 large, sweet oranges
frosted mint leaves or candied orange peel to decorate*

SYRUP
100 ml (80 g) granulated sugar
200 ml (⁴/₅ cup) water
1 stick cinnamon
3 cloves
10 ml (2 tsp) lemon juice
30 ml (2 tbsp) orange liqueur

Cut the oranges in half, horizontally, and then peel, removing all the white pith.
Make the syrup: place sugar, water, spices and lemon juice in a wide-based, heavy frying pan. Bring to the boil, stirring to dissolve sugar, then add oranges, arranging them flat sides down in a single layer. Cover, and poach gently for 15–20 minutes, until soft, basting occasionally. Using a slotted spoon, remove oranges to a serving dish to fit snugly in a single layer. Reduce syrup by boiling rapidly until very bubbly and just beginning to turn a pale caramel colour. Remove from stove, remove cloves and cinnamon, and add liqueur. Pour syrup over oranges, cool, cover, and chill for at least 4 hours. Just before serving, garnish with frosted mint leaves or candied orange peel.
Serves 4, or 8 if serving with ice cream.

* Dip single, perfect leaves of mint in lightly beaten egg white, then into castor sugar, and leave to dry; or cook julienned orange rind in a light sugar syrup until soft and caramelised.

ZUCOTTO POTS

A version of a luscious, Florentine dessert combining tipsy cake, cream, nuts and chocolate. Usually made in a dome-shaped mould, this method breaks with tradition in that it is made in individual ramekins, making it much easier to serve, and the little igloo-shaped zucottos are novel and attractive. Once the cake has been cut, the dessert is quick to assemble, and the recipe makes 12 miniatures.

2 uniced chocolate sponge cakes (buy for convenience)
60 ml (¼ cup) orange liqueur
45 ml (3 tbsp) brandy
60 g mixed, blanched almonds and hazelnuts
375 ml (1½ cups) cream
90 ml (6 tbsp) sifted icing sugar
a few drops of vanilla essence
100 g dark chocolate, grated or finely chopped
extra icing sugar to decorate

Slice sponges horizontally into 1 cm layers. Using a scone cutter stamp out 24 circles to fit the diameter of 12 small ramekins. Line each ramekin with a large circle of plastic wrap and nestle a round of cake in the base of each. Mix orange liqueur and brandy and drizzle 5 ml (1 tsp) over each round of cake.
Toast almonds and hazelnuts. Rub skins off hazelnuts and chop all nuts finely.
Whip cream with icing sugar and vanilla until very stiff. Fold in nuts and chocolate. Divide between ramekins, levelling tops. Place remaining circles of cake on top of cream and drizzle each with remaining liqueur and brandy. Pull up overhanging plastic wrap to cover, and chill in the refrigerator overnight.
Lift zucotto pots out and invert onto individual plates as you remove the wrap. Sift a little icing sugar over each, and serve with small dessert forks.
Serves 12.

BEST BAKED BANANAS

There's nothing new about a hot banana, but this easy recipe scores in that they are simply placed in a baking dish, drizzled with orange juice and other sweet things, and set aside to be baked at dinnertime. Serve with coffee or mango ice cream for an interesting mix of flavours, or top with a dollop of crème fraîche.

4 large, firm bananas (about 550 g)
lemon juice
30 ml (2 tbsp) soft brown sugar
125 ml (½ cup) fresh orange juice
2 ml (½ tsp) finely grated orange rind
10 ml (2 tsp) honey
30 ml (2 tbsp) orange liqueur
a pinch of ground cinnamon
30 ml (2 tbsp) desiccated coconut
butter

Peel bananas, slice in half lengthwise and pack tightly into a buttered dish to fit – a 20 cm pie dish is just right. Sprinkle with a little lemon juice and then with the brown sugar. Mix together orange juice, rind, honey, liqueur and cinnamon, and pour over bananas. Sprinkle with coconut and dot with just a few slivers of butter.

Cover, and set aside if working ahead. Bake, uncovered, at 180 °C for about 30 minutes, until bananas are soft and a toasted, golden brown. **Serves 4.**

CRÈME FRAÎCHE
Pour 250 ml (1 cup) cream into a sterilised glass jar. Mix in 30 ml (2 tbsp) buttermilk, close jar and leave in a warm place until thickened (1–2 days). Chill at least 1 day before using. Whip with 75 ml (5 tbsp) iced water to lighten if desired.

CHOCOLATE MERINGUE PIE

A silky smooth chocolate filling nestled in crisp meringue. The crust, flattish, not a Pavlova, may be made in advance and stored in an airtight container, then filled and refrigerated before serving.

CRUST
2 egg whites
a pinch of salt
a pinch of cream of tartar
125 ml (100 g) castor sugar
30 ml (2 tbsp) finely ground, toasted hazelnuts
a pinch of ground cinnamon

FILLING
100 g dark chocolate, broken
30 ml (2 tbsp) water
5 ml (1 tsp) cocoa powder
5 ml (1 tsp) instant coffee powder
200 ml (⁴⁄₅ cup) cream
2 ml (½ tsp) vanilla essence
chocolate curls to decorate

To make crust, whisk egg whites until foamy. Add salt and cream of tartar and whisk until stiff. Gradually add sugar, whisking constantly until mixture forms stiff peaks. Using a metal spoon, gently fold in ground nuts and cinnamon. Shape meringue on a baking tray lined with baking paper into a 20 cm circle, building up the sides to form a shell. Bake at 150 °C for 15 minutes, then at 120 °C for 1 hour. Switch off oven and leave until absolutely cold.

To make filling, melt chocolate, water, cocoa powder and instant coffee in a small container over low heat, stirring until absolutely smooth. Cool. Whip cream with vanilla until very stiff, then gently fold in chocolate mixture.

Spoon into crust, smoothing top with a dampened spatula. Refrigerate for 2–3 hours, then decorate with chocolate curls and serve in wedges. **Serves 8.**

CHOCOLATE TORTE WITH MOCHA CREAM

If a chocolate dessert torte can be modest, this is it – not too sweet, no butter, only one slab of chocolate – yet it's moist and dark enough to satisfy most chocaholics. Settle the slices on individual plates flooded with the liqueur-laced cream, and serve with small dessert forks.

5 eggs, separated (absolutely must be extra-large)
125 ml (100 g) castor sugar
a few drops of vanilla essence
45 ml (3 tbsp) cocoa powder
100 g dark chocolate, broken (not cooking chocolate)
5 ml (1 tsp) instant coffee powder
45 ml (3 tbsp) water
icing sugar and chocolate curls to decorate

MOCHA CREAM
250 ml (1 cup) cream
15 ml (1 tbsp) castor sugar
5 ml (1 tsp) instant coffee powder
coffee liqueur

Whisk egg yolks, sugar and vanilla until thick and creamy – the mixture should look like whipped butter. Place cocoa, chocolate, coffee powder and water in a small container and melt over low heat. Do not bring anywhere near boiling point, but stir once or twice to dissolve the cocoa – the mixture will be very thick. Use a spatula to scrape it out of the container, and add to the egg mixture in small dollops. Whisk until thoroughly combined. Using a metal spoon, fold in egg whites stiffly whisked with a pinch of salt.

Pour into an oiled 22 cm cake tin and bake on the middle shelf of the oven at 180 °C for 35 minutes, or until firm and the cake has pulled away from the sides of the tin. Cool in the tin – the cake will sink slightly in the centre, forming a 'nest', like a cheesecake.

Just before serving, softly whip cream, sugar, coffee powder and just enough liqueur to flavour delicately. Sift a little icing sugar over the top of the cake, and decorate with a few chocolate curls. Slice and present as suggested.
Serves 8.

INSTANT ICE CREAMS

Use an electric, hand-held whisk to whip up the following quick ice creams, which contain similar ingredients but have different flavours and textures. Once mixed, none of them requires any further beating or folding, but – as with most home-made ice creams – they do need to be allowed to soften slightly before serving.

VANILLA SNOW ICE CREAM
Sour cream cuts the sweetness of this basic ice cream, which makes a huge quantity and is perfect for serving with fruit salad.

500 ml (2 cups) cream
7 ml (1½ tsp) vanilla essence
1 x 397 g can condensed milk
250 ml (1 cup) cultured sour cream
5 egg whites, stiffly whisked with a pinch of salt

Whisk the cream with vanilla until stiff. Add condensed milk slowly while whisking. Continue whisking while gradually adding the sour cream. When it is thoroughly combined and thick, fold in the egg whites, using a metal spoon. Turn into a 2½ litre container and freeze. **Makes about 2½ litres.**

LEMON ICE CREAM
Make a fuss of the delicate flavour by serving this ice cream unadorned – simply pile small scoops into frosted champagne glasses and top with a sprig of mint or frosted mint leaves.

250 ml (1 cup) cream
15 ml (1 tbsp) very finely grated lemon rind
5 ml (1 tsp) vanilla essence
1 x 397 g can condensed milk
250 ml (1 cup) cultured sour cream
4 egg whites, stiffly whisked with a pinch of salt

Whisk cream with lemon rind and vanilla until stiff. Add condensed milk slowly while whisking. Continue whisking while gradually adding sour cream. When thoroughly combined and thick, fold in the egg whites, using a metal spoon. Turn into a 2 litre container and freeze. **Makes about 2 litres.**

ORANGE LIQUEUR ICE CREAM
Dress this ice with a fresh mango coulis as a gracious complement to the flavour.

500 ml (2 cups) cream
10 ml (2 tsp) very finely grated orange rind
5 ml (1 tsp) vanilla essence
45 ml (3 tbsp) orange liqueur
1 x 397 g can condensed milk
1 x 170 g can evaporated milk, chilled overnight
lemon juice
4 egg whites, stiffly whisked with a pinch of salt

Whisk cream with orange rind and vanilla until stiff. Add liqueur to condensed milk, stirring until combined.
Slowly add to cream while whisking. Whip evaporated milk until stiff, adding a few drops of lemon juice.
Fold into the cream mixture, then fold in the egg whites, using a metal spoon. Turn into a 2½ litre container and freeze. **Makes about 2½ litres.**

MANGO COULIS
1 large, fibreless mango, peeled and diced
about 75 ml (5 tbsp) orange juice

Place in a blender and blend until it is smooth and of a thick, pouring consistency.

To whip chilled evaporated milk successfully, chill the bowl, and beaters as well, before using.

TROPICAL BRÛLÉE WITH COCONUT CREAM

I am passionate about this dessert, which I devised for two reasons: firstly, to combine three wonderful fruits in a new guise and, secondly, to make a brûlée without a fridge-to-oven baking dish because one seldom has just the right size for a particular number of servings. The result is a do-ahead delight, accessible to any reasonably equipped cook.

**1 x 410 g can pitted litchis, well drained and sliced
2 large, fibreless mangoes, peeled and diced (400 g flesh)
pulp from 2 small granadillas
60 ml (¼ cup) orange liqueur
250 ml (1 cup) cream
60 ml (4 tbsp) toasted desiccated coconut*
soft brown sugar**

Combine the fruit and divide between 6 ovenproof ramekins. Drizzle 10 ml (2 tsp) orange liqueur over each, then cover each ramekin with plastic wrap, drape a kitchen towel over the lot, and set aside for up to 3 hours.
  Whip cream stiffly, fold in coconut, and refrigerate. Just before serving, heat oven grill. Spread the chilled cream in a thick, even layer over the top of each bowl of fruit, and sprinkle with a little sugar – do not use more than about 5 ml (1 tsp) on each serving as the dessert is sweet and the sugar is simply there to melt and look pretty. Set the ramekins under the hot grill for a few seconds until the sugar melts and serve at once.
Serves 6.

* Spread coconut thinly on base of a non-stick frying pan and toast on low heat, or spread on a baking tray and place in a low oven until golden brown.

MOCHA CREAM LOG WITH STRAWBERRIES

A rich, layered combination of orange-soaked biscuits wrapped around with cream, and topped with fresh strawberries to add colour and cut the decadence. Present on a large flat platter, and use a sharp knife to serve in slices.

125 ml (½ cup) fresh orange juice
2 ml (½ tsp) finely grated orange rind
1 x 125 g packet Boudoir biscuits
300 ml (1⅕ cup) cream
45 ml (3 tbsp) castor sugar
10 ml (2 tsp) pure instant coffee powder
30 ml (2 tbsp) coffee liqueur, preferably Kahlúa
strawberries, hulled and rinsed, for topping
strawberry jam for topping

Mix orange juice and rind in a large soup bowl. Moisten half of the biscuits with this mixture, turning them over several times until softened but not soggy. Shake off any drips and place side-by-side on a flat serving platter. Whip cream with sugar until very stiff. Dissolve coffee in liqueur and fold into cream. Spread a third of the cream over the biscuits. Dip the remaining biscuits in orange juice, and layer on top of the cream. Cover top and sides with remaining cream and refrigerate for at least 8 hours, preferably overnight.

Just before serving, halve strawberries and arrange on top, placing them in rows to facilitate slicing, and glaze with a little warmed, sieved strawberry jam. **Serves 6–8.**

When instant coffee powder is called for, use 100% pure instant coffee granules.

FRESH FRUIT FOOL

A more apt name for this recipe would simply be Slush or Mush, but neither sounds tempting, so Fool it is – the old-fashioned name for a purée of fruit and cream – and doubtless so called because they are so utterly simple to make. Fools are one of the best ways of ending a heavy meal. There are no rules – if you have a blender, some fruit and some cream, you have it made. The following combination of mangoes, pineapple and rum-flavoured cream is a delicious example. Serve on the day of making.

1 kg chopped mango flesh*
4 slices sweet ripe pineapple, cored and diced
10 ml (2 tsp) lemon juice
30 ml (2 tbsp) honey
about 125 ml (½ cup) fresh orange juice
125 ml (½ cup) cream
15 ml (1 tbsp) icing sugar
30 ml (2 tbsp) dark rum
a few drops of vanilla essence

Place mango flesh, pineapple, lemon juice and honey in a blender and blend to a smooth purée, adding just enough orange juice to provide a smooth result. Turn into a glass bowl with a lid – the mixture should fill the bowl – and cover and refrigerate for several hours.

Whip the cream with icing sugar until very stiff. Add rum and vanilla and whip again, then refrigerate.

To serve, spoon purée into individual dessert dishes or wide champagne glasses. Add a large dollop of cream to each, and swirl through. Alternatively, cover the top of each Fool with cream, or serve the cream separately for those who want a really refreshing dessert. **Serves 8.**

* As the size of mangoes varies, the weight is given for the peeled, pitted fruit. For the 1 kg mango flesh required here, you will need 3–4 large mangoes.

BAKED CHOCOLATE CHEESECAKE

This cheesecake is not as quick as the fluffy cheesecakes set with gelatine, but chocaholics will love the fudgy flavour. Biscuit crusts are the easiest, but if time allows, try the pastry base.

BISCUIT CRUST
250 ml (90 g) fine biscuit crumbs
75 ml (5 tbsp) melted butter
10 ml (2 tsp) cocoa powder

FILLING
250 ml (1 cup) cream
100 g dark chocolate, broken into pieces
10 ml (2 tsp) instant coffee powder
3 eggs
175 ml (140 g) castor sugar
500 g smooth, low-fat cottage cheese
5 ml (1 tsp) vanilla essence

Mix the ingredients for the crust and press onto the base of a greased 20 x 6 cm tin with a removable base. Bake in the oven for 10 minutes at 150 °C, and cool while mixing filling.

To make the filling, rinse a small saucepan with cold water (to prevent burning), then pour in cream. Add chocolate and coffee and heat very gently, stirring now and then, until chocolate softens and starts to melt. This takes a little while as the heat must be kept low. Do not worry if it does not smooth out completely – any little grains or flakes will disappear in the baking. Whisk eggs, sugar and cheese until smooth, then add the hot cream mixture and vanilla and whisk well.

Pour the mixture – which will be runny – into the tin and bake on the middle shelf of the oven at 150 °C for 1 hour 10 minutes. Turn off the oven heat, open the door slightly and leave the cheesecake undisturbed until cold, then chill overnight. (Expect a few cracks on top, and a slightly raised rim.) Serve plain, or decorate with chocolate curls. **Serves 8.**

PROCESSOR CRUST
Place 150 ml (70 g) cake flour, 15 ml (1 tbsp) cocoa powder, 15 ml (1 tbsp) castor sugar, 60 g diced, cold butter, 1 ml (¼ tsp) baking powder and a pinch of salt in a processor fitted with the metal blade. Process until the mixture forms a ball, press out onto the base of a greased tin, and bake at 180 °C for 15 minutes. Cool before adding the filling. **Serves 8–10.**

MOCHA-RUM CREAMS

This custard laced with coffee and rum makes a very rich, slightly tipsy dessert to set in elegant glasses.

15 ml (1 tbsp) gelatine
45 ml (3 tbsp) rum
375 ml (1½ cups) milk
10 ml (2 tsp) instant coffee powder
3 eggs, separated
90 ml (6 tbsp) granulated sugar
a large pinch of salt
2 ml (½ tsp) vanilla essence
125 ml (½ cup) cream, whipped
milk chocolate, shaved or grated, to decorate

Sprinkle gelatine onto rum and leave to sponge. Scald milk with coffee. Beat egg yolks, sugar and salt, add the hot milk, then return to saucepan and stir over low heat until thickened – do not boil. Remove from stove, stir in sponged gelatine and vanilla, then pour into a bowl and leave until cold but not set. Fold in cream and stiffly whisked egg whites, and pour into 6 glasses. Sprinkle with chocolate and refrigerate until set. **Serves 6.**

BATTER BREADS

Home-made bread rises to new heights in these plump, crusty loaves. Apart from the rising period, they are as quick to make as stirred breads as instant yeast requires no sponging and there's no kneading involved. The only causes of a flopped loaf are using too much or too little water, or water that is too hot (which will kill the yeast) or too cold (which won't activate it): it should be just hotter than lukewarm. It will take just one successful loaf, and you'll know you've got it right. As unbaked batter breads have a sticky consistency, they may be left to rise uncovered; however, if covering with a damp cloth or plastic wrap as with regular yeast breads, be sure to remove these before the batter reaches the top of the tin. Once baked and inverted onto a rack, rap the bottom with your knuckles – if it sounds hollow, the loaf is done. For easier inverting, stand briefly, then run a knife around the edges.

OLIVE AND WALNUT BATTER BREAD

An extravagant loaf with gourmet appeal to serve with pasta, pâtés or salads. For a less pricey loaf, use a bright red pepper instead of the chopped walnuts.

750 ml (360 g) white bread flour
5 ml (1 tsp) salt
5 ml (1 tsp) sugar
10 ml (2 tsp) instant dry yeast
4 spring onions, chopped, plus some tops
2 cloves garlic, crushed
12–16 green olives, pitted and slivered
60 g walnuts, coarsely chopped, or 1 small red pepper, seeded and diced
15 ml (1 tbsp) butter
about 375 ml (1½ cups) warm water
grated Parmesan cheese for topping

Sift flour with salt and sugar. Mix in yeast, onions, garlic, olives and walnuts, or red pepper. Melt butter in 250 ml (1 cup) of the water and stir into batter, then add remaining water, or enough to make a sticky, springy mixture, beating well with a wooden spoon.

Use a dampened spatula to press down and spread evenly into an oiled 19 x 8 x 7 cm loaf tin. (Do not use a smaller tin as the batter puffs up in the oven; a 20 x 10 x 7 cm tin may also be used, but the loaf will then not be quite as 'dumpy'.)

Sprinkle lightly with cheese and press in gently, then leave in a warm place for 45–60 minutes, until risen to the top of the tin. (This takes longer than usual due to the chunky ingredients.)

Bake at 200 °C for 30 minutes, reduce heat to 180 °C and bake for a further 15–20 minutes.

The loaf should have a crisp, deeply browned crust. Turn out and cool on a rack, and serve on the day of baking.

Makes 1 medium loaf.

HERBED BATTER BREAD

The most moreish bread – it could steal the limelight from any soup or salad, or just spread it with butter and eat it on its own.

750 ml (360 g) white bread flour
5 ml (1 tsp) each salt and sugar
10 ml (2 tsp) instant dry yeast
2 cloves garlic, crushed
60 ml (4 tbsp) chopped fresh herbs (parsley, sage, origanum, thyme, rosemary, chives: almost any ratio or combination will do)
15 ml (1 tbsp) butter
375 ml (1½ cups) warm water
sesame and/or poppy seeds for topping

Sift together flour, salt and sugar. Mix in yeast, garlic and herbs. Melt butter in 250 ml (1 cup) of the water and stir in, and then, while stirring with a wooden spoon, slowly add remaining water or just enough to make a springy, sticky batter. Stir

vigorously to combine and then, using a dampened spatula, spread evenly into an oiled 19 x 8 x 7 cm loaf tin. Sprinkle with seeds, patting in lightly. Leave in a warm spot until dough reaches the top of the tin, about 45 minutes.

Bake at 200 °C for 30 minutes, then reduce heat to 180 °C and bake for another 15–20 minutes. Stand for a minute before running a knife round the sides to loosen, and invert onto a rack to cool. Best served on the day of baking.

Makes 1 medium loaf.

When working with yeast, the temperature of the water is very important – it should be warmer than lukewarm, but not hot. Add the water slowly, using just enough to make a soft, but not slippery, batter.

HERBED FLAT BREAD

Round, flat breads are trendy at present, and are often served with a meal of pasta. Usually they require a spell of kneading, but in this quick version the ingredients are simply stirred together and the rising time is short. Flat breads should always be broken into chunks and served freshly baked.

500 ml (240 g) white bread flour*
10 ml (2 tsp) instant dry yeast
2 large cloves garlic, crushed
3–4 spring onions, chopped, plus some tops
a little chopped parsley
2 ml (½ tsp) dried origanum
2 ml (½ tsp) salt
5 ml (1 tsp) sugar
15 ml (1 tbsp) sunflower oil
about 250 ml (1 cup) warm water
3 sprigs fresh rosemary
grated Parmesan cheese

Mix all ingredients except the water, rosemary and cheese in a mixing bowl. Slowly stir in enough water to make a sticky dough, just elastic enough to be patted into a springy ball, using a wooden spoon.

Turn into a deep, 20 cm oiled cake tin with a removable base. Wet your fingertips and pat the dough out evenly.

Top with rosemary and cheese, pressing in lightly. If using a deep tin, drape a damp cloth over the top, otherwise leave uncovered, and stand until risen and puffy, about 35 minutes.

Bake at 200 °C for 25 minutes. The cheese will have melted to a stippled, brown topping, and the rosemary will be shrivelled and aromatic.

Turn out onto a rack to cool, removing base.

Makes 1 medium, flat bread.

* For wholewheat flat bread, use half white flour and half wholewheat flour.

VARIATIONS

✰ For a pizza-sized bread, use double the ingredients and bake in a 29 x 3 cm tin; if using a 22 cm cake tin, use 1½ times the ingredients.The baking time remains the same for both sizes.

✰ Add 30 g slivered sun-dried tomatoes and 6–8 sliced green olives to the pizza-sized recipe for the most stunning flat bread of all.

If substituting wholewheat flour for some of the white flour for extra fibre and less refinement, remember that you will probably need a little more water, and the bread will not rise as much.

BEST-EVER BUTTERMILK BREAD WITH HERBS

Whether served at a barbecue, a buffet, or simply with soup, this loaf will steal the limelight. It is very big and crusty, and plump with flavour. Best served slightly warm and thickly sliced.

4 x 250 ml self-raising flour (480 g)
250 ml (120 g) wholewheat flour
7 ml (1½ tsp) salt
5 ml (1 tsp) sugar
10 ml (2 tsp) mixed dried herbs*
3 cloves garlic, crushed
125 ml (½ cup) chopped parsley
2 pickling onions, finely chopped
2 medium sticks table celery, plus leaves, finely chopped
500 ml (2 cups) buttermilk
1 egg
about 125 ml (½ cup) water
grated Parmesan cheese for topping

Mix all ingredients except buttermilk, egg and water. Whisk buttermilk with egg, add to dry ingredients and stir to mix, adding just enough water to make a thick, sticky batter. The mixture is quite headstrong, and needs a strong wrist – use a wooden spoon and beat hard to combine thoroughly, then turn into an oiled 26 x 9 x 7 cm loaf tin, using a dampened spatula to pat in evenly. Sprinkle with Parmesan, pressing in lightly, and bake at 180 ˚C for 1 hour. Run a knife round the sides and invert onto a rack to cool.
Makes 1 large loaf.

* Substitute 5 ml (1 tsp) each dried origanum and thyme, or 60 ml (4 tbsp) chopped, fresh herbs, excluding parsley.

STIRRED WHOLEWHEAT YOGHURT BREAD WITH WHEATGERM AND RAISINS

A basic recipe for a nutritious loaf which requires no rising time – you simply stir and bake.

250 ml (120 g) white bread flour
7 ml (1½ tsp) salt
5 ml (1 tsp) bicarbonate of soda
750 ml (360 g) wholewheat flour
60 ml (4 tbsp) wheatgerm
90 ml (6 tbsp) seedless raisins
500 ml (2 cups) stirred Bulgarian yoghurt
15 ml (1 tbsp) sunflower oil
30 ml (2 tbsp) honey
about 60 ml (¼ cup) water
sesame, sunflower and/or poppy seeds for topping

Sift white bread flour with salt and bicarbonate of soda. Mix in wholewheat flour, wheatgerm and raisins. Whisk together yoghurt, oil and honey. Stir into flour mixture, then add just enough water to make a sticky dough.
Stir hard until thoroughly combined, then turn into an oiled 26 x 9 x 7 cm loaf tin, patting in evenly. Lightly press seeds into the top. Make a slight depression down the centre to prevent uneven rising, and bake at 180 ˚C for 1 hour. Loosen sides with a round-tipped knife and stand for 5 minutes before turning out onto a rack to cool.
Makes 1 fairly large loaf.

Always weigh or measure flour BEFORE sifting.

SAVOURY MAIZE MEAL MUFFIN BREAD

This is a fantastic, novelty flat bread. Light, with a soft, crumbly texture, it is never sliced or buttered, but served warm and broken into chunks. It is perfect for nibbling with soups, and replaces rice with dishes like chilli mince.

375 ml (180 g) self-raising flour
250 ml (150 g) fine white maize meal
5 ml (1 tsp) salt
5 ml (1 tsp) baking powder
15 ml (1 tbsp) castor sugar
3 cloves garlic, crushed
5 ml (1 tsp) mixed dried herbs
60 ml (4 tbsp) chopped parsley
1 small green pepper, seeded and finely chopped
1 small onion, coarsely grated
1 egg
375 ml (1½ cups) buttermilk
60 ml (¼ cup) sunflower oil
paprika for sprinkling

Sift together flour, meal, salt, baking powder and sugar. Mix in garlic, herbs and vegetables. Whisk together egg, buttermilk and oil, and pour into a well in the centre of the flour mixture. Mix very quickly and lightly until no traces of flour remain – the mixture will be very soft and spongy.

Pour into an oiled and base-lined 18 cm square tin, sprinkle with paprika, and bake on the middle shelf of the oven at 220 °C for 25 minutes. Stand for a minute before turning out onto a rack. Remove baking paper, and serve warm. If reheating, replace in the baking tin and warm through at 160 °C. Serves 6.

Paprika does not keep. It should be used only if fresh, so replace frequently.

DOUBLE QUICK BREAD

This jumbo loaf is so easy to make that it puts home-made bread within everyone's reach. Baking powder breads do not usually have smooth, rounded tops, so if it has a few crusty cracks, do not be dismayed, they simply add to the homespun aura.

500 ml (240 g) cake flour
7 ml (1½ tsp) salt
30 ml (2 tbsp) baking powder
500 ml (240 g) wholewheat flour
45 ml (3 tbsp) wheatgerm
250 ml (90 g) oats
45 ml (3 tbsp) sunflower oil
10 ml (2 tsp) brown vinegar
500 ml (2 cups) warm water
15 ml (1 tbsp) honey
sesame and poppy seeds for topping

Sift cake flour, salt and baking powder into a large bowl. Mix in wholewheat flour, wheatgerm and oats. Whisk together oil, vinegar, water and honey, add to flour mixture, and mix to a soft and sticky batter.

Turn into an oiled 26 x 9 x 7 cm loaf tin, pressing down levelly and right into the corners with the back of a dampened wooden spoon. Sprinkle with seeds in diagonal stripes, and bake at 180 °C for 1 hour. Turn out onto a rack to cool. Best served on the day of baking. **Makes 1 large loaf.**

Wheatgerm is the inner part of the grain and is rich in protein, and vitamins E and B in particular. Toasting it lightly improves its rather strange flavour. Raw wheatgerm must always be refrigerated.

ONE-BOWL CHOCOLATE SQUARES

375 ml (180 g) cake flour
250 ml (200 g) castor sugar
60 ml (4 tbsp) cocoa powder
7 ml (1½ tsp) baking powder
1 ml (¼ tsp) salt
125 g soft butter, diced
200 ml (⅘ cup) milk
60 ml (¼ cup) black coffee
2 eggs
5 ml (1 tsp) vanilla essence
45–60 g walnuts or pecan nuts, chopped

ICING
375 ml (190 g) icing sugar, sifted
30 ml (2 tbsp) soft butter, diced
15 ml (1 tbsp) cocoa powder
5 ml (1 tsp) instant coffee powder dissolved in 30 ml (2 tbsp) cold water
2 ml (½ tsp) vanilla essence
shaved chocolate to decorate

Sift flour, sugar, cocoa, baking powder and salt into a mixing bowl. Add butter, milk and coffee, and whisk on medium speed for 1 minute. Add eggs and vanilla, and whisk on high speed for 1 minute. Fold in nuts.

Pour into an oiled and base-lined 18 cm square tin, allowing mixture to spread evenly by shaking and tilting gently towards the corners. Bake on the middle shelf of the oven at 180 °C for 45 minutes – test with a skewer. Cool cake in the tin, on a rack. Turn out onto a cake plate.

To make icing, whisk all ingredients together until smooth. As the icing is quite firm, use a dampened spatula to spread over the top and sides of cake. Top with shaved chocolate, and cut into squares to serve.
Makes 12 large squares.

ONE-BOWL WHOLEWHEAT ORANGE SPICE CAKE

The addition of wholewheat flour makes this more wholesome than a white layer cake. It's not as light, but the flavour is super – and it also uses less butter.

375 ml (180 g) cake flour
375 ml (300 g) castor sugar
15 ml (1 tbsp) baking powder
2 ml (½ tsp) salt
5 ml (1 tsp) ground cinnamon
2 ml (½ tsp) ground mixed spice
250 ml (120 g) wholewheat flour
60 g soft butter, diced
60 ml (¼ cup) sunflower oil
10 ml (2 tsp) finely grated orange rind
250 ml (1 cup) milk
3 eggs
5 ml (1 tsp) vanilla essence

ICING
vanilla butter icing using 750 ml (390 g) icing sugar, flavoured with 2 ml (½ tsp) finely grated orange rind and moistened with orange juice instead of milk

Sift cake flour, sugar, baking powder, salt and spices into a large bowl. Mix in wholewheat flour. Add butter, oil, orange rind and milk. Using an electric beater, whisk on medium speed for 2 minutes. Beat the eggs with vanilla, add to the mixture and whisk on high speed for 1 minute.

Turn into two 20 cm oiled and base-lined tins and bake on the middle shelf of the oven at 180 °C for 30–35 minutes, until firm – the layers will be an unusually deep, toasted-brown colour. Cool for 5 minutes. Turn out onto a rack, remove paper and cool, then sandwich the layers with half the icing and spread the remainder on top.

ONE-BOWL NUTMEG AND HONEY CAKE

This is by no means a towering sponge – quick-mix cakes do not aspire to great heights – but it is beautifully moist, keeps well, and has a lovely flavour. Top with vanilla butter cream icing and serve in squares.

125 g very soft butter, diced
125 ml (100 g) castor sugar
60 ml (¼ cup) pale, thin honey
500 ml (240 g) self-raising flour
1 ml (¼ tsp) salt
7 ml (1½ tsp) grated nutmeg
2 ml (½ tsp) ground cinnamon
2 eggs (must be extra-large)
250 ml (1 cup) buttermilk
2 ml (½ tsp) vanilla essence
halved pecan nuts to decorate

Put all the ingredients into a mixing bowl in the above order. Using an electric whisk, beat for 1½ minutes on high speed – the batter should be thick and creamy, and the butter completely dissolved. Turn into a base-lined and oiled 20 cm square tin, using a spatula to spread evenly. Bake at 180 °C for 25–30 minutes. Invert onto a rack, remove paper and cool. Ice and decorate with halved pecan nuts.
Makes 16 squares.

Freshly grated nutmeg is far superior in flavour to ready-ground. Special little graters are available for this purpose.

VANILLA LAYER CAKE WITH BUTTERSCOTCH ICING

This cake makes a large, sweet contribution to a special-occasion tea. Once again, the batter is quickly mixed, using an electric whisk, but the icing requires more attention than usual.

60 g butter
60 ml (¼ cup) sunflower oil
250 ml (1 cup) milk
300 ml (240 g) castor sugar
3 eggs, separated
5 ml (1 tsp) vanilla essence
625 ml (300 g) cake flour
15 ml (1 tbsp) baking powder
1 ml (¼ tsp) salt

ICING
60 g butter
750 ml (390 g) icing sugar
2 ml (½ tsp) vanilla essence
milk and boiling water

Heat butter and oil together until butter has melted, pour into a mixing bowl, add milk, sugar, egg yolks and vanilla, and whisk well. Sift in flour, baking powder and salt, and whisk for 1 minute at high speed – the batter will thicken as the butter cools. Whisk the egg whites stiffly, and fold in.

Turn into two 20 cm oiled and base-lined tins, spreading evenly, and bake on the middle shelf of the oven at 180 °C for 25–30 minutes, until golden brown and firm. Stand for 1 minute before inverting onto a rack. Remove paper and cool.

To make icing, melt butter in a small pan and allow to bubble until caramel-coloured – be careful not to let it burn and darken. Add to icing sugar and vanilla, and whisk to combine, then gradually beat in a little milk and a little boiling water to make a creamy consistency. Use to sandwich layers and ice the top of the cake.

CHOCOLATE ORANGE LAYER CAKE

A big, dark cake with a gorgeous gaggle of flavours.

90 ml (6 tbsp) cocoa powder
5 ml (1 tsp) instant coffee powder
250 ml (1 cup) boiling water
10 ml (2 tsp) finely grated orange rind (1 large orange)
4 eggs, separated
375 ml (300 g) castor sugar
5 ml (1 tsp) vanilla essence
125 ml (½ cup) sunflower oil
500 ml (240 g) cake flour
15 ml (1 tbsp) baking powder
1 ml (¼ tsp) salt
chocolate curls to decorate

ICING
vanilla butter icing using 750 ml (390 g) icing sugar, flavoured with a little cocoa powder and instant coffee powder

Stir cocoa, coffee powder, water and orange rind together and leave to cool. Whisk egg yolks with sugar and vanilla until sugar has dissolved and mixture resembles creamy butter. Add cocoa mixture and oil, and whisk until combined. Sift in flour, baking powder and salt, and whisk briefly, just until smooth. Fold in stiffly whisked egg whites, using a metal spoon.

Pour into two 20 cm oiled and base-lined tins, and bake on the middle shelf of the oven at 180 °C for 25 minutes. Stand for a few minutes before inverting onto a rack. Remove paper and cool, then ice and decorate with chocolate curls.

> *When using orange rind to flavour cakes, biscuits or desserts, use firm but ripe oranges and a very fine grater – the result will be almost a pulp, and just a little will provide plenty of flavour.*

EASY-MIX CINNAMON CRUMBLE SPONGE

This whisked butter sponge is halved after baking, sandwiched with butter icing flavoured with cinnamon, and served in plump and delicious squares.

TOPPING
30 ml (2 tbsp) self-raising flour
5 ml (1 tsp) ground cinnamon
30 ml (2 tbsp) golden brown sugar
30 ml (2 tbsp) butter
45 ml (3 tbsp) finely chopped pecan nuts

SPONGE
500 ml (240 g) self-raising flour
a pinch of salt
5 ml (1 tsp) ground cinnamon
250 ml (200 g) castor sugar
125 g soft butter, diced
2 eggs
125 ml (½ cup) milk
5 ml (1 tsp) vanilla essence

Make topping by mixing flour, cinnamon and sugar. Rub in butter until crumbly, then mix in nuts and set aside. Place all ingredients for sponge in a large mixing bowl. Using an electric beater, whisk on high speed for 2–3 minutes, until absolutely smooth and creamy.

Turn into an oiled and base-lined 18 cm square tin, at least 5 cm deep, spreading evenly. Sprinkle the topping mixture over the batter, and bake on the middle shelf of the oven at 180 °C for 45 minutes.

Stand briefly before turning out onto a rack – the topping will have sunk into the cake while baking, making it possible to invert without losing any crumble – remove paper, and cool. Slice through the middle, horizontally, spread with icing (simply made by adding ground cinnamon and a few drops of vanilla to ordinary butter icing), then replace the top half.
Makes 16 large squares.

CARROT AND BANANA LAYER CAKE WITH PECAN NUT ICING

A king among carrot cakes: moist, wholesome, and lavished with nutty cream cheese icing. Irresistible at any time, and may even be served as a sweet dénouement at a brunch.

45 ml (3 tbsp) honey
200 ml (160 g) castor sugar
250 ml (1 cup) sunflower oil
2 eggs
250 ml (120 g) cake flour
5 ml (1 tsp) bicarbonate of soda
10 ml (2 tsp) baking powder
5 ml (1 tsp) ground mixed spice
a pinch of salt
250 ml (120 g) wholewheat flour
2 large, ripe bananas, mashed
3–4 carrots (200 g), coarsely grated
200 ml (120 g) fruit cake mixture
2 ml (½ tsp) vanilla essence

ICING
45 ml (3 tbsp) soft butter
625 ml (325 g) icing sugar, sifted
2 ml (½ tsp) ground cinnamon
about 75 ml (5 tbsp) cream cheese
a few drops of vanilla essence
45–60 g pecan nuts, chopped

Beat honey, sugar, oil and eggs until creamy. Sift in cake flour, bicarbonate of soda, baking powder, spice and salt, and whisk until combined, then mix in wholewheat flour. Add bananas, carrots, fruit cake mixture and vanilla, combining lightly but thoroughly.

Pour into two oiled and base-lined 20 cm cake tins, using a spatula to spread evenly. Bake on the middle shelf of the oven at 160 °C for 35–40 minutes, until risen, brown and firm. Stand for a few minutes, then invert onto a rack, remove paper and cool.

To make icing, cream butter with icing sugar and cinnamon. Using a wooden spoon, slowly beat in enough cheese to make icing spreadable. This takes a while, but it will soften – do not add any liquid. Add vanilla and nuts, and fill and ice the layers.

FLOP-PROOF FRUIT LOAF

Dark, sweet loaves are always popular. This loaf incorporates wholewheat flour and sunflower oil. Cut into slices to serve, and spread lightly with butter.

250 g fruit cake mixture
60 g pitted dates, chopped
a few glacé cherries, chopped
2 tea bags
250 ml (1 cup) boiling water
60 ml (¼ cup) sunflower oil
1 egg, beaten
250 ml (200 g) golden brown sugar
250 ml (120 g) wholewheat flour
250 ml (120 g) cake flour
10 ml (2 tsp) baking powder
10 ml (2 tsp) cocoa powder
2 ml (½ tsp) each salt, ground cinnamon, ginger and nutmeg
5 ml (1 tsp) vanilla essence
60 ml (¼ cup) milk

Place fruit and tea bags in a large bowl. Add water, stir to mix, then cover and leave overnight. Remove tea bags and mix in oil, egg, sugar and wholewheat flour.

Sift cake flour, baking powder, cocoa, salt and spices directly into mixture, add vanilla, fold everything together, then stir in milk. Combine lightly but well, turn into an oiled and floured 19 x 8 x 7 cm loaf tin, and bake on the middle shelf of oven at 160 °C for about 1¼ hours.

Test with a skewer and, if done, remove from oven and stand for a minute or two before turning out onto a rack to cool.
Makes 1 medium loaf.

> *Sunflower oil, or butter and oil, can often be used successfully in baking. The results may not be as moist or have the keeping qualities provided by butter, but this does cut down on saturated fat and is therefore healthier.*

RAISIN BREAD

This recipe makes home-made raisin bread accessible to everyone. As it is not a kneaded loaf, it will not be quite as light as shop-bought raisin bread – but it's a really big loaf, very fruity, deliciously spicy, and easy to slice. Serve fresh or toasted, lightly buttered.

500 ml (240 g) white bread flour
500 ml (240 g) cake flour
15 ml (1 tbsp) instant dry yeast
7 ml (1½ tsp) salt
7 ml (1½ tsp) ground cinnamon
2 ml (½ tsp) grated nutmeg
90 ml (6 tbsp) castor sugar
30 ml (2 tbsp) sunflower oil
250 ml (150 g) seedless raisins
60 ml (4 tbsp) cut mixed peel
about 450 ml (1⅘ cups) warm water
cinnamon-sugar for topping*

Mix all ingredients except water. Slowly stir in the water, using enough to make a soft batter. Mix well, then turn into an oiled and base-lined 26 x 9 x 7 cm loaf tin. Sprinkle with cinnamon-sugar, and leave to rise in a warm place for about 45 minutes or until the batter has risen to within 1 cm of the top of the tin. (The fruit and sugar will slow down the rising process somewhat.) Bake at 200 °C for 30 minutes, then reduce heat to 180 °C and bake for a further 15 minutes. The loaf will puff up and crack a bit in the oven, but settles down on cooling. Stand for a few minutes, run a round-tipped knife round the sides, turn out onto a rack, remove paper, and cool.
Makes 1 large loaf.

* Sift 5 ml (1 tsp) castor sugar with just a pinch of ground cinnamon – too much cinnamon will darken the loaf too much.

GLAZED SPICE LOAF

A plain loaf with a great flavour. Perk up the appearance by studding the glaze with cherries and almonds, or omit the glaze and simply serve lightly buttered – as this is not a moist loaf it is easily cut into thin slices or fingers.

125 g butter
60 ml (¼ cup) golden syrup
125 ml (100 g) granulated sugar
500 ml (240 g) cake flour
60 ml (4 tbsp) cornflour
10 ml (2 tsp) ground ginger
5 ml (1 tsp) ground cinnamon
2 ml (½ tsp) grated nutmeg
1 ml (¼ tsp) salt
1 egg, beaten
5 ml (1 tsp) bicarbonate of soda
125 ml (½ cup) milk, unchilled

GLAZE
250 ml (130 g) icing sugar
5 ml (1 tsp) ground ginger
10 ml (2 tsp) butter
30 ml (2 tbsp) hot water
halved glacé cherries and blanched almonds to decorate

Melt butter, syrup and sugar over low heat, stirring. Pour into a mixing bowl and sift flour, cornflour, spices and salt directly into the melted mixture. Whisk until smooth, then mix in egg. Dissolve bicarbonate of soda in milk, add to flour mixture, and whisk briefly to make a smooth, soft batter.

Pour into an oiled and base-lined 19 x 8 x 7 cm loaf tin, using a wet spatula to spread evenly. Bake at 160 °C for 1 hour. Turn out onto a rack, remove paper and cool.

To make glaze, sift icing sugar with ginger; melt butter in hot water; stir together until smooth and then slowly drizzle over cooled loaf, allowing it to run down sides. Press the cherries and almonds over top before the glaze sets.

Makes 1 medium loaf.

ORANGE COCONUT LOAF

This is rather like a Madeira cake: light, moist, and rich in butter and eggs. Serve plain, in dainty slices, for an elegant tea.

375 ml (180 g) cake flour
125 ml (60 g) self-raising flour
1 ml (¼ tsp) salt
125 ml (40 g) desiccated coconut
250 g soft butter
250 ml (200 g) castor sugar
10 ml (2 tsp) finely grated orange rind
4 eggs
30 ml (2 tbsp) cut mixed peel, finely chopped (optional)*
60 ml (¼ cup) fresh orange juice

Sift flours with salt, then mix in coconut. Cream butter, sugar and orange rind until light. Beat in eggs singly, adding 5 ml (1 tsp) flour mixture with each egg, and beating well between additions. If using cut peel, mix into remaining flour. Fold half into creamed mixture, combining lightly but thoroughly, then fold in orange juice, and finally fold in remaining flour.

Turn batter – which will be quite thick – into a very lightly oiled and base-lined 23 x 8 x 7 cm loaf tin, spreading lightly. Make a slight depression down the centre, then bake on the middle shelf of the oven at 160 °C for about 1 hour – test with a skewer, it might need a few minutes more. Stand for 5 minutes, turn out onto a rack, remove paper, and cool.

Makes 1 medium loaf.

*This is the packaged mixture, consisting of orange peel, lemon peel, glucose syrup, etc.

NUTTY FRUIT AND CARROT LOAF

Nutty as a fruit cake, this very moist, malt-coloured loaf contains a flurry of festive spices and carrots. Not meant for dainty nibbling, but sweetly satisfying served in thick slices, plain or buttered.

250 ml (200 g) golden brown sugar
125 g pitted dates, chopped
250 g fruit cake mixture
5 ml (1 tsp) each ground mixed spice and ground cinnamon
1 ml (¼ tsp) ground cloves
250 ml (1 cup) water
2 medium carrots, coarsely grated
30 ml (2 tbsp) butter
500 ml (240 g) cake or white bread flour
1 ml (¼ tsp) salt
60 g pecan nuts, chopped
5 ml (1 tsp) bicarbonate of soda
125 ml (½ cup) milk, unchilled

Place sugar, dates, fruit mixture, spices, water, carrots and butter in a large saucepan, stir to mix, bring to the boil, then cover and simmer for 5 minutes. Tip into a large mixing bowl and leave until cold.
　Sift in flour and salt, then mix in nuts. Dissolve bicarbonate of soda in milk and stir into mixture, combining well.
　Turn into an oiled and base-lined 26 x 9 x 7 cm loaf tin, make a slight depression down the centre, then bake at 160 °C for 1¼ hours. Turn out onto a rack, remove paper and cool.
Makes 1 large loaf.

Extra-large eggs have been used throughout. In most recipes, smaller eggs will not give satisfactory results.

CHOCOLATE, DATE AND GINGER NUT LOAF

A fudgy-dark teatime treat. Serve sliced and lightly buttered.

250 ml (1 cup) boiling water
250 g pitted dates, chopped
60 g soft butter
30 ml (2 tbsp) sunflower oil
250 ml (200 g) golden brown sugar
1 egg
2 ml (½ tsp) vanilla essence
500 ml (240 g) self-raising flour
30 ml (2 tbsp) cocoa powder
a pinch of salt
5 ml (1 tsp) ground ginger
1–2 knobs of preserved ginger, chopped
60 g chopped walnuts or pecan nuts

Pour water over dates and leave to cool, then mash roughly, using a wooden spoon. Whisk butter, oil, sugar, egg and vanilla together until light and creamy. Sift dry ingredients into mixture, fold together until thoroughly combined, then stir in the date mixture. Fold in chopped ginger and nuts. The mixture will be soft and tacky, rather like a chocolate cake batter.
　Turn into an oiled and base-lined 20 x 11 x 7 cm loaf tin, level top with the back of a wet spoon and make a slight depression down the centre.
　Bake on the middle shelf of the oven at 180 °C for 50–60 minutes, testing with a skewer. Turn out onto a rack, remove paper and cool.
Makes 1 medium loaf.

WHOLEWHEAT HONEYED BANANA LOAF

This is a moist, dense and really satisfying loaf. The addition of wholewheat flour is in line with the trend towards using unrefined ingredients in sweet, baked goodies, but those who prefer a lighter loaf could substitute white or plain brown flour, and an extra 50 ml (⅕ cup) sugar instead of the honey.

250 ml (120 g) cake flour
10 ml (2 tsp) baking powder
2 ml (½ tsp) bicarbonate of soda
a pinch of salt
5 ml (1 tsp) ground mixed spice
45–60 g pecan or macadamia nuts, chopped
125 ml (75 g) sultanas
250 ml (120 g) wholewheat flour
125 g soft butter
200 ml (160 g) castor sugar
30 ml (2 tbsp) honey
2 eggs, beaten
5 ml (1 tsp) vanilla essence
4 medium bananas, mashed

Sift together cake flour, baking powder, bicarbonate of soda, salt and spice. Add nuts, sultanas and wholewheat flour. Using an electric whisk, beat butter, sugar and honey until creamy. Whisk in eggs and vanilla, together with a spoonful of the flour mixture, then add bananas, whisking well. Fold in flour mixture, combining thoroughly.
  Spoon the batter – which will be soft and sticky – into an oiled and base-lined 26 x 9 x 7 cm loaf tin, levelling the top with the back of a wet spoon.
  Bake at 160 °C for about 1 hour 10 minutes, or until richly browned and a skewer inserted into the centre comes out clean. Invert onto a rack to cool. Serve sliced and buttered.
Makes 1 fairly large loaf.

EVERGREEN OATIES

Flop-proof cookies that have stood the test of time. The first recipe is for large, flat, eggless oaties with mixed fruit and wheatgerm. The second provides round, crinkly, spiced cookies with raisins. Both are nice and crunchy, and quickly made using an electric whisk.

1
250 g soft butter
250 ml (200 g) white sugar
375 ml (180 g) cake flour
1 ml (¼ tsp) salt
500 ml (180 g) oats
30 ml (2 tbsp) wheatgerm
250 ml (150 g) fruit cake mixture
5 ml (1 tsp) vanilla essence
2 ml (½ tsp) bicarbonate of soda
45 ml (3 tbsp) boiling water

Cream butter and sugar, sift in flour and salt, whisk well to combine, then mix in oats, wheatgerm, fruit cake mixture and vanilla. Dissolve bicarbonate of soda in water and mix everything to a soft and rather sticky ball. Use a grapefruit spoon to scoop up and place in rough heaps on oiled and lined trays, leaving room for spreading. Press down lightly with a fork and bake in the oven at 180 °C for 14–15 minutes. Stand to crisp for a few minutes, then transfer to a rack to cool, using a spatula. Makes 36.

2
125 g soft butter
250 ml (200 g) golden brown sugar
250 ml (120 g) cake flour
5 ml (1 tsp) baking powder
5 ml (1 tsp) ground cinnamon
1 ml (¼ tsp) salt
2 ml (½ tsp) bicarbonate of soda
1 egg
5 ml (1 tsp) vanilla essence
500 ml (180 g) oats
125 ml (75 g) small, seedless raisins

Cream butter and sugar, sift in flour, baking powder, cinnamon, salt and bicarbonate of soda, and whisk to a soft, crumbly mixture. Beat egg with vanilla and mix in, then stir in oats and raisins. Mix to a soft ball, then pinch off pieces and roll into balls, flouring palms occasionally. Place on oiled and lined trays, leaving room for spreading, press down with a fork, and bake at 180 °C for 20 minutes. Stand to crisp for a few minutes, then use a spatula to transfer to a rack to cool. Makes 30.

MUNCH BARS

Sweet and spicy bars with bran cereal, wholewheat flour and sunflower seeds adding their particular nuttiness and flavour.

125 g butter, melted
250 ml (200 g) granulated sugar
250 ml (120 g) cake flour
5 ml (1 tsp) baking powder
a pinch of salt
2 ml (½ tsp) bicarbonate of soda
5 ml (1 tsp) ground cinnamon
2 ml (½ tsp) grated nutmeg
1 egg
2 ml (½ tsp) vanilla essence
250 ml (120 g) wholewheat flour
250 ml (45 g) All-Bran flakes, coarsely crushed
125 ml (40 g) desiccated coconut
60 ml (4 tbsp) sunflower seeds
60 ml (4 tbsp) currants

Cream butter and sugar. Sift in flour, baking powder, salt, bicarbonate of soda and spices, and mix. Add egg beaten with vanilla and blend well, then stir in remaining ingredients. Combine well, press firmly and evenly into an oiled 25 x 20 cm tin, and bake at 180 °C for 25 minutes. Slice into bars, but leave until cold before removing. Makes 25.

BISCUITS

BUTTERSCOTCH BUTTONS

Delicate, short and rich biscuits with a fudgy flavour.

250 g very soft butter
250 ml (200 g) golden brown sugar
5 ml (1 tsp) vanilla essence
500 ml (240 g) cake flour
125 ml (60 g) cornflour
5 ml (1 tsp) baking powder
a pinch of salt

Cream butter, sugar and vanilla very well. Sift in remaining ingredients, and whisk until mixture combines to make a soft dough. Shape into a ball, pinch off pieces, press flat with the heel of your palm (if they stick, dampen your hand now and then) and place on lined but not greased baking trays, leaving room for spreading. Using a fork, prick each biscuit twice to make 6 holes, like a button.

Bake on the middle shelf of the oven at 160 °C for 15–17 minutes, until pale beige in colour – do not allow to brown. Leave on trays to crisp for a few minutes before removing with a spatula to a rack to cool.
Makes 36.

These recipes have been devised for those who like the idea of home-made cookies, but who have no time to roll, cut, chill, or even decorate. In almost all cases an electric hand-held whisk is used for mixing. This makes short work of creaming, but it does mean that the butter should be really soft, or it will not cream well enough to melt the sugar. In several recipes I have used sunflower oil in order to cut down on the quantity of butter, and wholewheat flour and oats to add fibre.

OAT AND COCONUT CHOC-SNAPS

Irresistible old favourites.

125 g soft butter
250 ml (200 g) golden brown sugar
1 egg, beaten
2 ml (½ tsp) vanilla essence
125 ml (60 g) cake flour
5 ml (1 tsp) baking powder
a pinch of salt
20 ml (4 tsp) cocoa powder
125 ml (60 g) wholewheat flour
250 ml (90 g) oats
125 ml (40 g) coconut

Cream butter and sugar. Mix in egg and vanilla. Sift in cake flour, baking powder, salt and cocoa. Whisk to combine, then mix in wholewheat flour, oats and coconut. Shape into a ball – the dough will be soft – pinch off pieces and roll into balls.

Place on oiled and lined trays, leaving room for spreading, and press down lightly with a fork – you will need to dip it into flour occasionally to prevent sticking. Bake in the oven at 180 °C for 12 minutes. Use a spatula to remove to a rack to cool.
Makes 30.

Baking paper is not the same as greaseproof or waxed paper. The one I use is a pure vegetable parchment without additives. Place the printed side down, away from the food.

NUTTY DOUBLE GINGERS

Crinkly, rotund cookies with preserved ginger and nuts making them quite different from ordinary gingersnaps.

250 g soft butter
250 ml (200 g) golden brown sugar
1 egg, beaten
2 ml (½ tsp) vanilla essence
750 ml (360 g) self-raising flour
25 ml (5 tsp) ground ginger
a pinch each of ground cloves and salt
60–90 g pecan nuts, finely chopped*
30 ml (2 tbsp) finely chopped preserved ginger

Cream butter and sugar. Add egg and vanilla, and beat well. Sift in flour, ground ginger, cloves and salt. Mix well, then add nuts and ginger and shape into a ball. Pinch off pieces, roll into balls and place on oiled and lined trays. Press down with a fork, then bake at 180 °C for about 18 minutes until pale brown. Cool on a rack.
Makes 40.

* This is a flexible weight as nuts are expensive, and with biscuits the amount used can safely be left to the cook.

CINNAMON CURRANT CRACKLES

Golden brown, large, crisp cookies with a scrumptious flavour.

60 g soft butter
60 ml (¼ cup) sunflower oil
250 ml (200 g) castor sugar
1 egg, beaten
250 ml (120 g) cake flour
2 ml (½ tsp) baking powder
2 ml (½ tsp) bicarbonate of soda
a pinch of salt
7 ml (1½ tsp) ground cinnamon
125 ml (60 g) wholewheat flour
125 ml (45 g) oats
90 ml (6 tbsp) currants

Cream butter, oil and sugar, then mix in egg. Sift in cake flour, baking powder, bicarbonate of soda, salt and cinnamon, and whisk. Add wholewheat flour, oats and currants, and mix to a soft dough. Shape into a ball, pinch off pieces, and roll into balls. Place on oiled and lined trays, leaving room for spreading, and flatten lightly with a fork – you will need to dip the fork into flour now and then as the dough is very soft. Bake at 180 °C for 12–14 minutes, then remove, using a spatula, and cool on a rack.
Makes 28.

CHOCOLATE MUESLI CRISPIES

Large, dark, flat and very munchy cookies.

250 g soft butter
250 ml (200 g) castor sugar
250 ml (120 g) cake flour
30 ml (2 tbsp) cocoa powder
a pinch of salt
750 ml (270 g) untoasted, unsweetened muesli
5 ml (1 tsp) vanilla essence
2 ml (½ tsp) bicarbonate of soda
30 ml (2 tbsp) hot water

Cream the butter and sugar. Sift in the flour, cocoa and salt. Whisk to combine, then mix in the muesli and vanilla – use a wooden spoon here as the mixture is too sticky to whisk. Dissolve the bicarbonate of soda in the water and mix in. Combine together well to make a soft ball.

Pinch off pieces, roll into balls, and place on oiled and lined baking trays, leaving room for spreading.

Flatten with a fork, then bake on middle shelf of the oven at 180 °C for 10 minutes. Leave on trays for a few minutes to crisp. Use a spatula to transfer to a rack to cool.
Makes 40.

RUM TRUFFLES

*To make decadent but dead-easy rum truffles to serve with after-dinner coffee, melt 125 g butter with 100 g dark chocolate. Sift in 250 ml (130 g) icing sugar and stir until smooth. Add 500 ml (180 g) **very** fine Marie biscuit crumbs and 30 ml (2 tbsp) rum. Remove from the stove and mix in 60 ml (¼ cup) cream.*

Spread 1,5 cm thick in a buttered dish. Mark into squares and refrigerate.
Makes 32.

SPICY BROWN SUGAR BISCUITS

250 g butter
250 ml (200 g) golden brown sugar
1 egg, beaten
2 ml (½ tsp) vanilla essence
750 ml (360 g) self-raising flour
10 ml (2 tsp) ground cinnamon
2 ml (½ tsp) grated nutmeg
a pinch of ground cloves
a pinch of salt

Cream butter and sugar. Add egg and vanilla, and whisk until combined. Sift in remaining ingredients, mix to a dough, pinch off pieces and roll into balls. (The dough will be soft, but should be rollable between the palms.) Place on lined baking trays leaving room for spreading, press down twice with a fork, and bake at 180 °C for about 18 minutes, until pale brown. Cool on a rack.
Makes 40.

NUTTY PROCESSOR SHORTBREAD

There's a tiny shop on a damp little island off the west coast of Scotland which sells the finest shortbread I've ever eaten. Back home, I devised the following recipe using an electric whisk for speed, and the result is as close as I can get to that wonderful nutty shortbread from Mull.

125 g soft butter
75 ml (5 tbsp) castor sugar
300 ml (150 g) cake flour
75 ml (5 tbsp) cornflour
30 g finely chopped walnuts or pecan nuts
extra castor sugar for topping

Whisk butter and sugar very well until creamy. Sift in both flours and whisk well, then shape into a ball with your hands, turn out and knead in the nuts.

Press firmly into an ungreased 20 cm round layer cake tin, decorate around the edge with the tines of a fork, score across lightly into 8 segments, and prick well with the fork.

Bake on the middle shelf of the oven at 150 °C for 45 minutes. Cut through segments and dust liberally with extra castor sugar. Leave in the tin until cold, then remove slices carefully and store in an airtight container.
Makes 8 wedges.

VARIATION
To make Shortbread Fingers, make a double quantity and press into an ungreased 32 x 22 cm Swiss roll tin. Prick all over, score into 27 strips, then continue as above.

BROWN SCONES WITH FRUIT AND MARMALADE

Sweet and satisfying scones, using half wholewheat flour and half cake flour to lighten them a bit. Serve straight from the oven for a lazy Sunday breakfast – all you need is butter and a jug of orange juice.

250 ml (120 g) cake flour
20 ml (4 tsp) baking powder
1 ml (¼ tsp) salt
30 ml (2 tbsp) castor sugar
5 ml (1 tsp) ground cinnamon
250 ml (120 g) wholewheat flour
60 g butter
125 ml (75 g) fruit cake mixture
60 ml (¼ cup) milk
30 ml (2 tbsp) water
5 ml (1 tsp) lemon juice
1 egg
30 ml (2 tbsp) orange marmalade

Sift together cake flour, baking powder, salt, sugar and cinnamon. Add wholewheat flour, rub in butter until crumbly, then mix in fruit. Whisk together remaining ingredients, and add to flour mixture. Using a fork, mix quickly and lightly until combined – the dough will be soft and sticky. Turn onto a floured board, pat out, and use a 5 cm cutter to cut out rounds – you will have to flour both your hands and the cutter.

Place on an oiled tray lined with two layers of baking paper, and bake towards top of oven at 220 °C for 14–15 minutes.
Makes 10.

Scones made with wholewheat flour don't rise much, so don't expect them to be light and fluffy. They are, though, more satisfying and wholesome than their cake flour counterparts.

SESAME OAT BARS

Mix in the morning and then bake for afternoon tea. These are crunchy, golden chews made with just a handful of wholesome ingredients.

500 ml (180 g) oats
250 ml (200 g) golden brown sugar
10 ml (2 tsp) ground ginger
45 ml (3 tbsp) lightly toasted sesame seeds
125 ml (½ cup) sunflower oil
1 egg, beaten
1 ml (¼ tsp) salt
2 ml (½ tsp) vanilla essence
extra sesame seeds for topping

Place oats, sugar, ginger, sesame seeds and oil in a mixing bowl, stir until well mixed and moist, then stand for at least 4 hours. Beat in egg, salt and vanilla, and, when thoroughly combined, press into an oiled 25 x 16 cm tin. (Although the mixture will be oily, it is necessary to oil the tin lightly or removal will be difficult.) Use a dampened wooden spoon to press down firmly and evenly. Sprinkle with sesame seeds and press in lightly.

Bake at in the oven at 160 °C for 30–35 minutes, until firm and a toasty beige colour.

Cut into oblong bars and leave in the tin until cold before removing.
Makes 20.

Because sweet, buttery biscuits tend to end up with burnt bottoms, especially if your oven heats up from the base element, I usually have used commercial, non-stick baking paper for lining, which requires no greasing and keeps your trays and tins clean. However, different types of bakeware give different results, and I therefore play it safe by first oiling the trays or tins, and THEN lining them – even when you are using non-stick ware.

INDEX

Amaretto
  cheesecake pots, with cherries 66
  with fruit salad, rainbow 67
Apple crumble, with muesli 69
Avocado
  purée, with fillet steaks 28
  relish, with tomato 52
  salad, with marinated
    mushrooms 9
  salad, with tomato and
    coriander 55
  soup, emerald summer 17
  soup, with cucumber and
    yoghurt, chilled 14

Baby marrows
  salad, with mushroom,
    in creamy dressing 54
  soup, with melted brie 18
  with mushrooms in cream 62
Bananas
  baked 72
  wholewheat loaf, with honey 89
Beans
  green, and corn, with
    cumin-sesame butter 63
  salad, three-bean,
    Mediterranean 56
Beef
  casserole, one-step 29
  curry, spicy mince
    and lentil 30
  fillet steaks, crumbed, with
    avocado purée 28
  rosemary sauce with sun-dried
    tomatoes, for steaks 28
  steaks, with red wine and
    mushroom sauce 30
Biscuits
  butterscotch buttons 91
  choc-snaps, with oats
    and coconut 91
  cinnamon currant crackles 92
  double gingers, with nuts 92
  muesli crispies, with chocolate 92
  munch bars 90
  oat bars, with sesame 94
  oaties, evergreen 90
  scones, brown, with fruit
    and marmalade 94
  shortbread, with nuts 93
  shortbread fingers 93
  spicy brown sugar 93
  truffles, rum 93
Breads
  batter, herbed 78
  batter, olive and walnut 78
  buttermilk, with herbs 80
  double quick 81
  flat, herbed 79
  maize meal muffin, savoury 81
  raisin bread 86
  wholewheat yoghurt, stirred,
    with wheatgerm and raisins 80

Brinjals
  casserole, with veal and olives 31
  honeyed, with peppers 37
  ratatouille, one-step 62
  stuffed, with ratatouille 49
  to dégorge 63
Bulgur
  salad, with rice 55
  tabbouleh, Lebanese 59
Butternut
  baked, orange 63
  baked, spiced 63

Cakes
  carrot and banana,
    with pecan nut icing 86
  chocolate orange 84
  chocolate squares 82
  nutmeg and honey 83
  sponge, with
    cinnamon crumble 84
  vanilla, with butterscotch icing 83
  wholewheat orange spice 82
Calamari
  goulash, with mushrooms 25
  starter, stir-fried,
    with vegetable salad 10
Carrots, honeyed ginger 62
Casserole
  beef, one-step 29
  lamb, Italian 33
  lamb, with mushrooms
    and butter beans 32
  veal, with brinjals and olives 31
Cauliflower
  salad, with leek and radish 58
  with creamy lemon dressing 64
Cheesecake
  baked, chocolate 77
  gelatine, to set 66
  litchi and ginger 69
  pots, cherry amaretto 66
  pots, chocolate orange 67
  pots, strawberry 66
Chicken
  almond, in creamy mustard
    and whisky sauce 39
  chutney, with orange 38
  coq au vin, orange 34
  curry
    tropical, with cream 36
    spicy 36
  Eastern, with mushrooms
    and coriander 40
  flambéed, in creamy garlic
    and mustard sauce 34
  in apple and mustard
    cream sauce 41
  low-kilojoule, with
    chunky vegetables 39
  marsala 40
  mykonos, with honeyed
    peppers and brinjals,
    and glazed baby onions 37
  salad, pineapple-sesame 41
  salad, walnut, with
    coriander yoghurt 35
  stir-fry, with litchis and ginger 38

Chickpeas
  curry, with mushroom
    and apple 50
  hummus, quick 13
Chillies, to handle 33
Chocolate
  biscuits
    choc-snaps, with oats
      and coconut 91
    muesli crispies 92
  cake
    with orange 84
    squares 82
  cheesecake
    baked 77
    pots, with orange 67
  loaf, with dates, ginger
    and nuts 88
  meringue pie 72
  torte, with mocha cream 73
  zucotto pots 71
Coulis
  mango 74
  strawberry 66
Couscous
  fragrant 65
  salad 65
  spinach, with almond risotto 52
Crème fraîche 72
Curry
  chicken, spicy, supreme 36
  chicken, in curry cream 36
  chickpea, mushroom
    and apple 50
  fish, simple 22
  salad, with rice, apple
    and walnut 60
  spicy mince and lentil 30

Desserts
  apple crumble, with muesli 69
  bananas, baked 72
  brûlée, tropical,
    with coconut cream 75
  cheesecake
    baked, chocolate 77
    litchi and ginger 69
    pots, cherry amaretto 66
    pots, chocolate orange 67
    pots, strawberry 66
  fruit salad
    Arabian, with honeyed cream 68
    rainbow, with amaretto 67
  fruit fool, fresh 76
  ice cream, instant
    lemon 74
    orange liqueur 74
    vanilla snow 74
  meringue pie, with chocolate 72
  mocha cream log,
    with strawberries 76
  mocha-rum creams 77
  oranges, poached, in liqueur 71
  strawberries, tipsy,
    with clove-scented cream 70
  torte, chocolate,
    with mocha cream 73
  zucotto pots 71

Fish
  baked, in chunky
    mushroom sauce 24
  baked, saucy,
    with crumb topping 26
  baked, sesame 20
  baked, with tomatoes
    and basil butter 21
  chilli, paprika 27
  curry, simple 22
  goulash, calamari
    and mushroom 25
  kingklip, almond, with
    pernod and parsley butter 24
  low-kilojoule, extra easy 22
  salmon, cutlets,
    with Italian-style sauce 25
  salmon, smoked, with pasta,
    mushrooms and cream 43
  spiced, in chilli-tomato sauce 23
  starters
    calamari, stir-fried,
      and vegetable 10
    salmon, smoked,
      with green bean salad 8
    salmon, marinated, smoked,
      and cucumber salad 8
    salmon, smoked, dip 12
  with almond and fennel
    butter sauce 27
  with mustard and caper
    cream sauce 26
  with stir-fried vegetables 21
Fruit salad
  Arabian, with honeyed cream 68
  rainbow, with amaretto 67

Ginger
  biscuits with nuts 92
  loaf, with chocolate and dates 88
Goulash, calamari
  and mushroom 25

Haricot beans, with tomatoes
  and mushrooms 50

Icing
  butterscotch 83
  pecan nut 85

Kingklip, almond, with pernod
  and parsley butter 24

Lamb
  casserole, Italian 33
  casserole, with mushrooms
    and butter beans 32
Lentils
  curry, with spicy mince 30
  Lebanese 48
  salad
    with rice 49
    with rice and mushroom 61
  soup, aromatic dhal 19

INDEX

Mocha
  cream log, with strawberries 76
  cream, with chocolate torte 73
  creams, with rum 77
Mushrooms
  casserole, with lamb
    and butter beans 32
  curry, with chickpeas
    and apple 50
  goulash, with calamari 25
  marinated 57
  with fettucine
    and sun-dried tomatoes 43
  with pasta, smoked salmon
    and cream 43
  with panzerotti and
    white wine sauce 45
  pasta sauce, with basil
    and cream 45
  salad
    with baby marrows,
      in creamy dressing 54
    with rice and sprouts 60
    with rice and lentils 61
  sauce, chunky, with baked fish 24
  sauce, with red wine,
    for beef steaks 30
  soup, Oriental, quick 17
  starters
    salad, marinated,
      with avocado 8
    mountains, Italian 11
    pâté, and cream cheese 12
    pâté, and
      chunky chicken liver 13
  with baby marrows, in cream 62
  with Eastern chicken,
    and coriander 40
  with haricot beans
    and tomatoes 50

Onions
  baby, glazed 37
  soup, French 16
Oranges, poached, in liqueur 71

Pasta
  fettucine, garden vegetable
    and herb 42
  fettucine, with mushrooms
    and sun-dried tomatoes 43
  herbed, with
    stir-fried vegetables 44
  panzerotti, with mushroom
    and white wine sauce 45
  salad, puttanesca 42
  salad, with herbed vegetables 47
  sauce, mushroom, basil
    and cream 45
  sauce, nutty Ricotta, tomato
    and pesto 45
  with smoked salmon, mushrooms
    and cream 43
Pâté
  chicken liver, chunky,
    and mushroom 13
  mushroom and cream cheese 12

Pesto
  de luxe 46
  economical 46
  for all seasons 46
Polenta, cheesy baked 53
Pork, chops, in apple sauce 31
Potatoes
  new, baked, with onions
    and garlic 64
  salad, with corn 59
  stuffed, with spinach
    and Ricotta 52

Ratatouille
  one-step 62
  stuffed brinjals 49
Rice
  brown, baked,
    with vegetables 65
  risotto, almond, with
    spinach couscous 52
  salad
    curried, with apple
      and walnut 60
    with bulgur 55
    with lentils 49
    with lentils and mushroom 61
    with mushrooms and sprouts 60
Rum truffles 93

Salad dressings
  basic blender 60
  mustard cream 64
Salads
  cauliflower, leek and radish 58
  chicken
    pineapple-sesame 41
    and walnut,
      with coriander yoghurt 35
  curried rice, apple and walnut 60
  for all seasons,
    with Italian dressing 56
  green, with fresh herbs 58
  mushroom and baby marrow,
    with creamy dressing 54
  mushrooms, marinated 57
  pasta
    puttanesca 42
    with herbed vegetables 47
  potato and corn,
    with mustard dressing 59
  rice and bulgur 55
  rice and lentil 49
  rice, lentil and mushroom 61
  rice, with mushrooms
    and sprouts 60
  starters
    calamari, stir-fried,
      and vegetables 10
    mushroom, marinated,
      and avocado 9
    salmon, marinated, smoked
      and cucumber 8
    salmon, smoked,
      with green beans 8
    timbales, red pepper,
      with green salad 9

stir-fried, with sesame 57
tabbouleh, Lebanese 59
three-bean, Mediterranean 56
tomato, avocado
  and coriander 55
vegetable, fresh,
  with vinaigrette 54
Salmon
  cutlets, with Italian-style sauce 25
  marinated, smoked,
    with cucumber salad 8
  smoked, dip 12
  smoked, with pasta 43
  smoked, with green bean salad 8
Sauce
  mustard, sherried,
    for lamb and beef 33
  pasta, nutty Ricotta, tomato
    and pesto 45
  pasta, mushroom, basil
    and cream 45
  pesto, de luxe 46
  pesto, economical 46
  pesto, for all seasons 46
  rosemary, with
    sun-dried tomatoes, for beef 28
Snacks, *see* Starters
Soups
  baby marrow, and melted brie 18
  broth, beef and barley,
    Granny's 19
  cucumber, avocado
    and yoghurt, chilled 14
  dhal, aromatic 19
  emerald summer 17
  gazpacho, quick,
    with basil cream 15
  Lisa's 16
  mushroom, Oriental,
    quick low-kilojoule 17
  onion, French 16
  pea, quick 16
  spinach, speedy 18
  vichyssoise, apple and celery 14
Soya beans, Oriental 48
Starters
  dips
    anchovy and green pepper 12
    chilli cumin 12
    herb, fresh 12
    mustard and garlic 12
    salmon, smoked 12
    sesame 12
  mushroom mountains, Italian 11
  pâtés
    chicken liver, chunky,
      and mushroom 13
    mushroom and cream cheese 12
  salads
    calamari, stir-fried,
      and vegetable 10
    mushroom, marinated,
      and avocado 9
    salmon, marinated, smoked,
      and cucumber 8
    salmon, smoked,
      and green bean 8
    timbales, red pepper,
      with green salad 9

spreads
  hummus, butter bean 13
  hummus, quick 13
Stir-fry
  chicken, with litchis
    and ginger 38
  salad, with sesame 57
  vegetables, with apple juice
    and garlic butter 51
  vegetables, with fish 21
  vegetables, with pasta 44
Strawberries
  cheesecake pots 66
  tipsy, with
    clove-scented cream 70
  with mocha cream log 76
Sunflower seeds, to prepare 55
Sweet loaves
  banana, wholewheat honeyed 89
  chocolate, date
    and ginger nut 88
  fruit, flop-proof 86
  glazed spice 87
  nutty fruit and carrot 88
  orange coconut 87
  raisin bread 86

Toasts
  French bread, with thyme
    and lemon butter 9
  sesame and garlic 10
Truffles, rum 93

Veal, casserole,
  with brinjals and olives 31
Vegetarian
  brinjals, stuffed,
    with ratatouille 49
  curry, creamy chickpea,
    mushroom and apple 50
  haricot beans, with tomatoes
    and mushrooms 50
  lentils, Lebanese 48
  polenta, cheesy baked 53
  potatoes, stuffed,
    with spinach and Ricotta 52
  risotto, almond, with
    spinach couscous 52
  salad, rice and lentil 49
  soya beans, Oriental 48
  vegetables, stir-fried,
    with apple juice and
    garlic butter 51

Yeast, to use 79